How to Draw Aircraft Like a Pro

Andrew C. Whyte, ASAA with text by **Charlie and Ann Cooper**

MBI Publishing Company

First published in 2001 by MBI Publishing Company Galtier Plaza, Suite 200, 380 Jackson Street, St. Paul, MN 55101-3885 USA

Motorbooks International books are also available at discounts in bulk quantity for industrial or sales-promotional use. For details write to Special Sales Manager at the Publisher's address MBI Publishing Company, Galtier Plaza, Suite 200, 380 Jackson Street, St. Paul, MN 55101-3885 USA

Library of Congress Cataloging-in-Publication Data Available

ISBN 0-7603-0960-4

Front cover, A finely detailed drawing of an A-4 Skyhawk. ©*Andy Whyte, ASAA*

Frontispiece
F-4 Phantom jets fly in formation over their aircraft carrier in this McCall painting. ©*Robert McCall,* ASAA

Title page
In this study, U.S. pilots scramble for their cockpits in the midst of the Japanese bombing attack of Pearl Harbor. ©*Robert McCall, ASAA*

Back cover, top
Mission Regensburg dramatically portrays the navigator and bombardier in their cramped front section of a B-17. ©*Gil Cohen, ASAA*

Back cover, bottom
Understanding how basic aircraft controls work allows you to depict an airplane accurately in any flight attitude. ©*Andy Whyte, ASAA*

Edited by Mike Haenggi
Designed by Katie Sonmor

Printed in China

CONTENTS

FOREWORD 6

INTRODUCTION, *Sergei Sikorsky* 12

CONTRIBUTING ARTISTS .14

CHAPTER 1   AERODYNAMICS AND ART 20

CHAPTER 2   THE TOOLS OF THE TRADE 34

CHAPTER 3   CONSIDERATIONS IN DRAWING AIRCRAFT 40

CHAPTER 4   SKETCHING AND LINE DRAWING 46

CHAPTER 5   REFERENCE AND RESEARCH MATERIALS 56

CHAPTER 6   GETTING THE RIGHT PERSPECTIVE 62

CHAPTER 7   CUTAWAYS AND SCALE VIEWS,

                COCKPITS AND INTERIORS 76

CHAPTER 8   CARTOONS AND *AEROCATURES*™ 84

CHAPTER 9   LIGHT AND SHADOW .90

CHAPTER 10   COMPOSITION 98

CHAPTER 11   COLOR 108

CHAPTER 12   CREATING PAINTINGS .116

GALLERY OF ARTISTS 126

GLOSSARY 154

BIBLIOGRAPHY 156

INDEX 158

FOREWORD

n the short 100 years since the first powered flight at Kitty Hawk, North Carolina, the aircraft has played a number of roles on the world stage. It has evolved into a primary means of commercial transportation, bringing people together, shrinking once formidable travel times, and delivering high-priority cargo around the globe swiftly and safely. Aircraft have become a valued transport for personal and corporate use, often demonstrating the adage that "the shortest distance between two points is a straight line."

Aircraft have served millions of hobbyists, who would rather build them than fly them, and training planes have been used to expand the numbers of pilots who will fly for careers or simply for fun. Barnstormers and aerobatic pilots have provided introductions to aviation that have thrilled and inspired generations of future pilots and showcased new aircraft designs for hundreds of thousands. Aircraft are widely used in agriculture, in surveying, and in providing utility line surveillance in rural areas. They have played a significant role in emergency services—fighting fires, assisting weather forecasters, and serving as high-speed ambulances. Aircraft have served the police and the traffic reporter, the doctor and the journalist. And, aircraft have become a primary weapon of war as well as of peacekeeping, attacking targets, delivering troops, and helping refugees.

Each of these varied and valuable roles has influenced aircraft designers as they work to meet the needs of the situation and the customer. Must the proposed craft fly faster—or slower? Must it reach higher or fly longer? Must it withstand the rigors of aerial combat, landing on short, unimproved fields, or the heaving decks of aircraft carriers? How many people must it safely transport or how much weight

➤ Montgolfier Brothers Hot-Air Balloon, France, 1783. ©Andy Whyte, ASAA

← Wright Brothers' 1903 Flyer, where it all began. ©*Andy Whyte, ASAA*

↓ Sikorsky S-42, the first aircraft to explore Pacific and South American routes for Pan American. ©*Andy Whyte, ASAA*

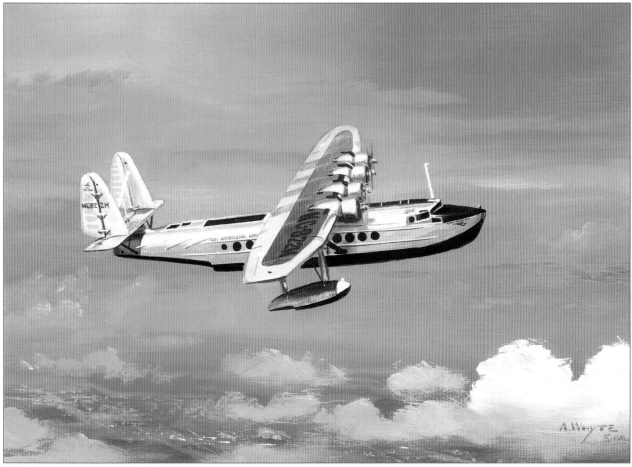

Launching the X-1 at Edwards AFB, California for Chuck Yaeger's flight through the sound barrier. ©Andy Whyte, ASAA

must it efficiently carry—in cargo, munitions, or fuel? How many "Gs"—equivalent forces of gravity, positive and negative—must the design aircraft safely sustain? What special needs must it meet? Will it be used for spraying crops or dropping retardant on forest fires? Must it be able to be reconfigured to carry cargo one day and ambulatory and bedridden wounded the next? Are the materials necessary to fulfill each of these needs available or is new technology required? Is the manufacturing capability to use the correct materials to meet the design requirements available or must new methods be devised?

The wide variety of aircraft designs that has resulted from the continuing quest to answer these hard questions satisfactorily has, over these same 100 years, resulted in an enormous variety of aircraft types. Each has sought, in its moment, to be the best craft for its purpose—the best transport, the best aerobatic aircraft, the best fighter, the best trainer, the best rescue vehicle, the best crop-duster—ever devised. Each has had its moment on the world stage; some have been stars, some have been in the chorus, and others have received bad reviews from the critics and have faded from the scene quickly. All have been replaced by new actors— younger, faster, capable of greater heights and longer flights, able to stand

more weather and more G forces—who, after their moments have passed, have faded too; gone perhaps, but never forgotten by those who have admired their style and grace and their ability to play the part.

Among the admirers of these succeeding generations of aircraft types are the aviation artists, the men and women who love to draw aircraft. Some draw aircraft and spacecraft for fun, to meet the challenges inherent in depicting rapidly moving, three-dimensional, widely varied objects on a two-dimensional surface. Others draw aircraft as a profession, striving continually to use the tools of their trade to make better pictures and to meet the demands of the markets they work to serve. Some focus their artistic efforts on imaginative futuristic interplanetary vehicles, some on modern jet transports, others on military aircraft of an earlier day. While always seeking perfection in their drawings and compositions, some aviation artists provide intensely detailed and accurate backgrounds for their paintings while others concentrate the viewer's attention solely on the aircraft itself. Depictions of weather conditions, of clouds and storms, are uniquely important to aviation artists as are the abilities to project the "bird's-eye view" and the speeds that are characteristic of aircraft.

↑Space exploration launch at Cape Canaveral, Florida. ©Andy Whyte, ASAA

Aviation artists share some basic understandings as they approach their art, their craft. They understand basic aerodynamics, the forces (lift, weight, thrust, and drag) and axes of flight (roll, pitch, and yaw), and the control surfaces of the aircraft that enable movement around those axes. This understanding enables the artist to show the distinguishing characteristics of a static aircraft on the ground as opposed to an aircraft in flight. It also provides the underpinning for the accuracy and consistency that become the hallmarks of the successful artist. Aviation artists understand the tools of their trade and the ways in which they can be used to achieve the desired effect in their drawings and, later, paintings. They understand the essential elements of sketching and line drawing like line weights, perspective, and values. They understand where they can get references and research materials and the contributions and limitations of photography and models—human and airplane. Above all, and with universal consistency, they understand that the path to perfection in drawing is to DRAW, DRAW, DRAW!

The focus of this book, then, is drawing, starting from the basics! The first elements of drawing discussed are perspective and ellipses, the essentials of depicting three-dimensional objects on a two-dimensional surface, whether those objects are made of flat or curved surfaces. Some methods of establishing correct perspective are discussed and attention paid to drawing cylindrical and curved objects, like wheels and tires and propeller arcs. Light and shadow become particularly important in drawings of aircraft because the out-of-doors, where aircraft operate, contributes great complexity of light sources, and shadows play a key role in establishing the shapes and settings of aircraft drawings. An understanding of values and the value scale enables the artist to do a great deal within the context of a drawing to convey depth, to create atmosphere, to focus attention, and to maintain interest. Having addressed perspective and ellipses, light and shadow, the discussion moves on to composition, the blending of the elements to make a drawing that conveys a meaning, tells a story. Every drawing has a purpose; some are quickly done to establish an idea on paper, others are finished works, with all of the focus and detail the artist wishes to include. Each has a foreground, a middle ground, and a background; "thumbnail" sketches help the artist put the three in perspective and to plan for the final drawing.

Color—hue, value, and intensity or saturation—permits the aviation artist to develop even the finished drawing to another level of complexity. Here, too, there is variety in the tools of the trade that permits different effects and presentations. Each tool and its general use will be briefly described. The book will then consider some of the different purposes for which aviation art is used and the distinct focus that can be brought by that art—cutaway drawings and scale views for engineering and advertising purposes, cartoons for humor and editorial point-making, paintings for illustrative purposes and fine art renditions. Each has a purpose, each has technique, and each expresses the artist's point of view. Each is based upon an ability to draw and a joy and passion for drawing well.

In drawing, as in many other aspects of living, perfection is approached only through practice. This book provides examples of the work of aviation artists—and Andy Whyte in particular—who draw airplanes like pros. They do it because they love it. Some of them make a very good living at it. Some teach others because, through teaching, they enhance their own skills. Some do it as a hobby, a sidebar to another successful career. All of them will tell you that their next drawing—or painting—will be better than anything they've done before. And so they follow the advice that we hope will be the essence of this book.

If you want to draw airplanes like a pro, you must DRAW, DRAW, and DRAW. Have fun while you're at it!

INTRODUCTION

Sergei Sikorsky

he challenge and the beauty of flight is a subject that has occupied mankind for tens of thousands of years. In ages long past, flight was the exclusive privilege of gods and angels, or supernatural creatures and demons. Then, some 100 years ago, the Wright Brothers flew and an impossible dream suddenly became reality.

Shortly after the birth of the airplane, the first poets, writers, and artists began to record their impressions of this new, exciting, and beautiful experience . . . the wonder and drama of flight. I feel, however, that it wasn't until the mid-1930s that aviation literature and aviation art came of age with the arrival of a new generation who knew aviation both professionally and artistically. I grew up reading the works of Charles and Anne Lindbergh and Antoine Saint-Exupéry, memorizing "High Flight," studying the artwork of Charles Hubbell, Clayton Knight, and Frank Tinsley of "Air Trails." Intoxicating stuff for a teenager hopelessly in love with aviation!

In World War II, the combat artists of the warring nations documented what the camera missed, often producing a visual impact that no photograph could duplicate. And who can ever forget the images created by the Army's Bill Mauldin in "Up Front," the USAAF's Bob Stevens doing his hangar flying in "There I Was. . .," and Bob Osborn's "Dilbert" and "Grandpa Pettibone," for those of us in naval aviation?

Today the aviation artist faces the challenge of painting for an audience that is far more experienced in aviation than was the case before World War II. As a result, the rapidly growing field of aviation art has bred a new generation who grew up exposed to aircraft and flight. Some engineers, while designing an aircraft, can predict by "feel" if a subtle change in a wingtip or a rudder fairing could increase the speed of the aircraft . . . or make it uncontrollable in a stall. Some pilots have a "sixth sense" when looking at an aircraft for the first time, and can predict the handling qualities even before flying it. And a gifted few can put that feel and sixth sense onto a piece of canvas and make it fly.

Three such gifted people have combined their professional and artistic skills to create the book *How to Draw Aircraft Like a Pro*: Andy Whyte and Charlie and Ann Cooper. Andy was born in Bridgeport, Connecticut, and grew up with a love of aviation inspired by his father, who served in the Royal Flying Corps and later in the Royal Air Force. Andy spent World War II in Naval Aviation as a flight engineer/

gunner in SBDs, PBYs, PBMs, and PV-2s and then in the reserves for a total of 10 years.

Andy Whyte attended the University of Oklahoma, majoring in mechanical engineering, and then joined Sikorsky Aircraft in 1951 in the Advanced Design Group. He combined engineering and art to produce configuration studies and, later, hundreds of paintings for Sikorsky Engineering and for marketing efforts during the past 38 years. Since retiring from Sikorsky, he has continued his painting, both for Sikorsky Aircraft and a growing number of other clients.

Ann Cooper is an accomplished author and writer, with some five books and over 700 magazine articles to her credit. She has written for such magazines as *Private Pilot, Sport Pilot, Kitplanes,* and *Aviation History*. Ann is the editor of *Aero Brush*, the quarterly magazine of the American Society of Aviation Artists. She has been a rated pilot for over 30 years, currently a Certificated Flight Instructor, Instrument Rated, with over 2,000 flight hours.

Charlie Cooper entered the Air Force in 1955 and retired as a Major General in 1991 with well over 4,000 hours logged as an Air Force Master Navigator. After a five-year tour of active duty, he joined the New York Telephone Company in 1960, then AT&T, and finally Bell Communications Research. He joined the New York Air National Guard in 1962, rose rapidly through operations and command positions, and served for seven years as Commander of the New York Air National Guard, the largest state organization in the Air National Guard. He is a member of numerous aviation-related organizations and a member of the U.S. Air Force Museum Foundation Board of Managers, as well as being the co-author, with Ann, of *Tuskegee's Heroes*, their first published book together.

The list of contributing artists is most impressive and includes many of the leading talents active in the aviation art scene here in the United States. To all of us interested in the history of aviation, and the art that documents that history, this book will be a valuable source of inspiration. To Major General and Mrs. Cooper, my sincere thanks. To a very good friend and fellow Naval Aircrewman Andy Whyte . . . a sincere "Well Done!"

—*Sergei Sikorsky*
  Surprise, Arizona

CONTRIBUTING ARTISTS

The authors are eager to express their gratitude to the many people who have contributed to and supported the development of this book. Of special note are the generous cooperation and gracious contributions of more than 30 of America's outstanding aviation artists. Each is a "Top Brush" in his or her own right and we are truly grateful to all of them. Although much could be written about each, space precludes the inclusion of more than the following limited biographies.

Richard Allison, ASAA* – Rolla, Mo. An Artist Fellow member of the American Society of Aviation Artists (ASAA), Richard is the former editorial cartoonist for Army Times Publishing Co., in Washington, D.C. He is a teacher, freelance artist, and an active participant in the Air Force Art Program. As a "historian with a paintbrush," Richard chronicles historic aviation and seeks to transmit the emotion of aviation to his viewers.

Gerald Asher, ASAA – Fort Worth, Tex. The oldest son of an Air Force mechanic and corporate pilot, Gerry has followed in his father's footsteps and has added a distinct talent for aviation art, completing many commissioned works. Employed today by American Airlines, he devotes his limited free time to his family, his research, and his painting. He is an active member of the Air Force Art Program and the ASAA.

Chad S. Bailey – Butler, Pa. Chad earned a BFA at the University of Utah and an MEd at the University of Phoenix. Adept with an airbrush and with brushes, Chad focuses on modern and World War II aircraft as well as naval vessels and has been widely published. He has recently completed art work for a Time-Life book on Pearl Harbor. An Artist Member of ASAA and participant in the Air Force Art Program, his greatest accomplishment is his family.

Paul Burrows – Summerville, S.C. Paul is a graduate of Virginia Polytechnic Institute and completed a commercial art course. A former Air Force and Air National Guard pilot, Paul retired in 1986 and now pursues an active career in art. He has painted book covers for major publishers and commissioned paintings for private collectors. He is an Artist Member of ASAA and an active airplane home-builder who flies his own plane.

Hank Caruso – California, Md. Hank's *Aerocatures*™ occupy a special niche in aviation art. In addition to his professional career as an aerospace test engineer, he is an award-winning artist. He has flown often with U.S. Air Force and Navy operational and test crews and has a complete understanding of the aircraft he depicts. His unique work is published as prints and calendars and in his book *Seabirds*.

John Clark, ASAA – Milwaukee, Wis. A past president of ASAA, John is an Artist Fellow. He served with the Air Force in

Southeast Asia and is currently on the staff of the University of Wisconsin, Milwaukee. John assisted Keith Ferris in the painting of a National Air and Space Museum mural and has judged the Experimental Aircraft Association (EAA) Art Competition. His award-winning work has been commissioned by NASA, the Air Force Art Program, and *Astronomy* magazine.

Gil Cohen, ASAA – Doylestown, Pa. A longtime teacher of art, Gil has been a strong proponent of the depiction of the human figure in all of his outstanding art. His commissioned work for the National Park Service, his numerous book covers, and his many commissioned paintings for private collectors tell their stories through the people involved. An award-winning artist, he is an active participant in the Air Force Art Program.

Domenic DeNardo, ASAA – Cranston, R.I. A professional artist, engineer, and pilot, Domenic has widely exhibited and has earned many awards for his paintings. He is an active member of the EAA, the Air Force Association, the Aircraft Owners and Pilots Association, and ASAA. Domenic's successful art career has spanned more than 40 years.

James Dietz, ASAA – Seattle, Wash. An outstanding story-teller in his art, Jim is the first EAA Master Artist and was the first to have a one-man show of his work at the EAA AirVenture Museum in Oshkosh, Wisconsin. Jim's paintings have been exhibited throughout the country and have won major awards in juried exhibitions. They are on display at many aviation museums and hang in many private collections.

Alex Durr – Fort Worth, Tex. Alex is a graduate of Florida State University with a degree in fine arts. A former USMC fighter pilot who now flies for American Airlines, he puts a "pilot's perspective" into each of his award-winning paintings. He is an Artist Member of ASAA and a participant in the Air Force Art Program. He has exhibited his work in numerous venues, including the EAA, the U.S. Air Force Museum, and the U.S. Naval Museum.

Jack Fellows, ASAA – Seattle, Wash. Jack is a past president of ASAA. As chairman of the Cactus Air Force Art Project, much of Jack's work has been focused on World War II in the Pacific. His paintings have been widely commissioned by military organizations and individuals and have earned him prestigious awards. His paintings have been featured in a wide variety of aviation publications and prints of his art enjoy wide distribution.

Keith Ferris, ASAA – Morris Plains, N.J. A founder and past president of the ASAA and an honorary U.S. Air Force *Thunderbird* who has logged more time in Air Force and Navy combat aircraft than many pilots, Keith has been a leader in the aviation art community for many years. In addition to his paintings, prints, advertisements, and magazine covers, he is best known for his two 75-foot murals at the National Air and Space Museum, Smithsonian Institution, Washington, D.C.

Nixon Galloway, ASAA – Manhattan Beach, Calif. An experienced professional, Nick is well known for the wide scope of the aviation art he has produced for a range of corporate clients and, more recently, for the paintings and prints he has created. He is a past president of the ASAA and has served as the Air Force Chairman for the Society of Illustrators, Los Angeles. His work is on display throughout the United States and internationally.

Luther Gore – Charlottesville, Va. The longtime executive secretary of the ASAA and professor at the University of Virginia, Luther has been an exemplary leader in aviation art. Through his initial efforts to bring artists interested in aviation together, the ASAA was born. Now retired, he is carrying his mark of excellence forward into his paintings.

Konrad F. Hack, ASAA – Niles, Ill. As a combat artist, he documented the Vietnam war. Konrad is now a professional artist and college-level teacher of art. A signature member of the Oil Painters of America/Representational and founder of the Midwest Air Force Art Program, he has done extensive work for NASA, for ASAA, and for professional sports teams. His award-winning work is displayed in museums and private collections.

Kristin Hill, ASAA – Lancaster, Pa. Kristin received her fine arts training at her alma mater, Mary Washington College, in Virginia. With family ties to aviation and diverse flight experiences, Kristin has specialized in aviation art for 25 years. Her prize-winning oil paintings hang in museums, corporate offices, and private collections. She has exhibited in numerous juried shows and is active in the Air Force Art Program.

Wilson Hurley, ASAA – Albuquerque, N.Mex. A graduate of West Point and an Air National Guard fighter pilot who served as a forward air controller in Vietnam, Wilson practiced law before turning to his art full-time. His work, for which he has been called "landscapist of grandeur," is perhaps best exemplified by his outstanding murals at the National Cowboy Hall of Fame in Oklahoma City. His award-winning aviation art is often based upon his own flying experiences.

Walter Matthews Jefferies – Hollywood, Calif. Matt has had a long and distinguished career as an aviation artist. A World War II veteran of the North African and Italian campaigns, he has been a corporate illustrator, a researcher at the Library of Congress, and an art director for motion pictures and TV series including *Star Trek* and *Little House on the Prairie*. He has been a rated pilot for 51 years, flying his own Waco. Matt has achieved renown as the designer of the *Starship Enterprise* for *Star Trek*.

John Paul Jones – El Paso, Tex. An artist, illustrator, historian, and pilot, John Paul has had a long involvement in aviation. His work has been exhibited at major museums and has appeared in a wide variety of books, magazines, and journals. He has received awards from the National Air and Space Museum, at ASAA Forums, and from the EAA in Oshkosh, Wisconsin. An ASAA Artist Member, he has been an art director and teacher.

James Laurier, ASAA – Keene, N.H. Jim graduated with honors from the Paier School of Art, Connecticut, and has completed commissioned art in diverse art genre. A trustee of the ASAA and an experienced private pilot, Jim has garnered awards from many galleries and museums for his carefully researched paintings. He is a member of the Society of Illustrators, the American Fighter Aces Association, and the Air Force Art Program.

Dorothy Swain Lewis – Idyllwild, Calif. An artist, teacher, and World War II Women's Airforce Service Pilot (WASP), Dot Lewis has created bronze sculptures honoring her WASP flying mates at the U.S. Air Force Academy, the Air Force Museum, Avenger Field, and the Confederate Air Force Museum. Her drawings and cartoons illustrated the first book about WASPs and her official portrait of the U.S. Attorney General has recently been unveiled.

Robert McCall, ASAA – Paradise Valley, Ariz. A founder of ASAA, Robert has been described as "the nearest thing to an artist in residence from outer space." He has chronicled the U.S. space program from its earliest days and has looked to the future and to the earliest past in imaginative paintings and murals, the best known of which is the six-story "The Space Mural, A Cosmic View" at the National Air and Space Museum.

Priscilla Messner-Patterson – Kodiak, Alaska. An active member of the ASAA, the Air Force and Coast Guard Art Programs, the Alaska Watercolor Society, and the Canadian Society of Aviation Artists, Priscilla has work displayed in private collections, including the Alaska Aviation Heritage Museum. Her work has focused on aviation-related scenes from Alaska, many of which feature floatplanes.

Michael O'Neal – North Brunswick, NJ. An avid researcher, Mike has specialized in painting highly accurate and prize-winning scenes of World War I aviation. His paintings have been recognized with top awards from the League of World War I Aviation Historians, the SimuFlite/*Flying* magazine, and ASAA annual juried shows. Mike is an Artist Member of ASAA and currently serves as chair of the scholarship committee.

Mark Pestana – Tehachapi, Calif. The son of a career Air Force crew member, Mark has served for over 20 years as an active-duty and Air Force Reserve pilot. Currently with the Flight Research Center in California, he flies NASA's DC-8 Flying Laboratory. He is an Artist Member of ASAA, a participant in the Air Force Art Program, an award-winning artist, and the designer of eight space shuttle mission patches.

William S. Phillips, ASAA – Ashland, Ore. Bill is an active member of the Air Force, Navy, and NASA Art Programs and he has received many top awards for his paintings including the Naval Aviation Museum's R. G. Smith Award. He has traveled extensively documenting aviation history and his paintings are in museums and private and public collections throughout the world. His nostalgic prints and his stamps have been top sellers.

Sharon Rajnus – Malin, Ore. Sharon's aviation art, which is displayed in collections and exhibitions across the country, focuses on historical moments in aviation history. Sharon earned her degree with majors in science, biology, and art; and she paints in watercolor and oil. Her aviation and wildlife art, which has been published in books and magazines, has won numerous awards and commissions. A pilot, she is an Artist Member of ASAA.

Paul Rendel, ASAA – Pittsburgh, Pa. Paul is a storyteller in his paintings, which often depict dramatic moments in history and in the lives of those who fly. A pilot and past president of ASAA, his prize-winning work hangs in collections throughout the United States. An EAA Master Artist, he has also won awards from the Naval Aviation Museum at Pensacola, Florida. Paul flies his own home-built, a two-place Thorp T-18.

John Sarsfield – Longmont, Colo. An Artist Member and officer of ASAA, John is an Air Force Academy graduate with a degree in aeronautical engineering. He has flown over 2,000 hours in combat aircraft, principally F-4s, and his early artwork focused on military jets. More recently, he has depicted historic and sport aircraft in scenes in which the setting is as important as the machine.

Jody Fulks Sjogren, ASAA – Lenexa, Kans. A member of an active aviation family, Jody began her professional career as a medical illustrator. In her aviation art, she has become best known for two series of paintings and prints: Metamorphoses and Metaphors. Both demonstrate and integrate her keen interests in nature, religion, and aircraft. An officer of ASAA, Jody is also a member of the Society of Illustrators.

Robert G. Smith, ASAA – Rancho Mirage, Calif. A founder of the ASAA, the late R. G. Smith had distinguished careers in aircraft design, for Douglas Aircraft for 50 years, and in art. His aviation art, which has been displayed in America's most prestigious museums and earned numerous major awards, has been rivaled only by his western art, paintings of rural America and Native Americans. A combat artist who served with the Navy in Vietnam, R. G. Smith is now immortalized at the Naval Aviation Museum with the award that bears his name.

Robert Watts, ASAA – El Cajon, Calif. Bob is a professionally educated artist and illustrator who works now as a freelance painter. He describes himself as one who has developed "a fine-art attitude in parallel with the engineering discipline." A Navy combat artist during the war in Vietnam, he has also developed a strong sense of combat operations. His award-winning art is displayed throughout the United States. Bob was the founding president of the Society of Illustrators in San Diego.

Andrew C. Whyte, ASAA – Norwalk, Conn. Andy was a U.S. Navy flight engineer/gunner during World War II, having been inspired by his father, an officer in the Royal Flying Corps during World War I. After his education in mechanical engineering in Oklahoma, Andy returned to Connecticut and joined Sikorsky Aircraft as a design engineer. He combined engineering and art in his configuration work at Sikorsky for 41 years. Now retired, Andy is an active freelance artist who is the president of ASAA and an active participant in the Air Force Art Program and the Society of Illustrators.

* ASAA following the artist's name denotes Artist Fellow member of the American Society of Aviation Artists.

The authors would like to express their appreciation to the owners and staff at McCallisters, the Midwest's most complete art supply store, in Dayton, Ohio, for their cooperation with this book. The store is amazing in the scope of its inventory.

And, finally, the authors would like to express their appreciation to MBI Senior Aviation Editor Mike Haenggi, whose idea led to the creation of this book. We trust that his interest and support will be rewarded.

AERODYNAMICS AND ART

The Wright Brothers To The Raptor

eronautical design *is* something that any other engineering discipline can do for twice the weight."
Andy Whyte, ASAA

WHY DO AIRCRAFT FLY?

Aircraft fly thanks to airfoils—the wings, tail surfaces, canards, and rotors—that use the movement of air flowing over and beneath their surfaces to create lift. Lift plus power (thrust) from an engine or engines combine to overcome the natural forces of weight (gravity) and drag. All aircraft have the same opposing forces: lift and thrust versus weight and drag.

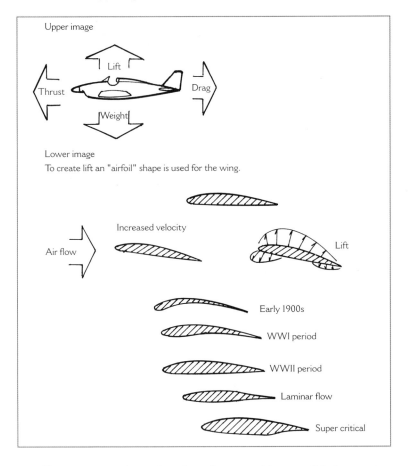

➤ (Upper Image) – All aircraft must deal with the same opposing forces: *lift* to overcome *weight* and allow the craft to move upward, and *thrust* to overcome the forces of *drag* and allow the craft to move forward.
©*Andy Whyte, ASAA*

(Lower Image) – Wings and rotors are built in *airfoil* shapes in order to create *lift.* Airflow follows the upper contours of the airfoil, with increased velocity over the upper surface, and is deflected downward at the trailing edge. Airflow coming into contact with the lower portions of the airfoil is also deflected downward. In accord with the laws of physics, these downward deflections result in an opposite, upward, reaction and *lift* is created. *Airfoil* shapes have evolved over time. ©*Andy Whyte, ASAA*

If you want to draw aircraft well, start with a careful observation of the shapes involved in your aircraft of choice and observe the way light strikes the airfoil shapes and the shadows that are cast.

AXES OF MOVEMENT IN FLIGHT

As aircraft are designed to move through the atmosphere and into the far reaches of outer space, they are designed to move through three axes—pitch, roll, and yaw. To understand the terms, picture yourself as the pilot and relate movement to that position in the cockpit.

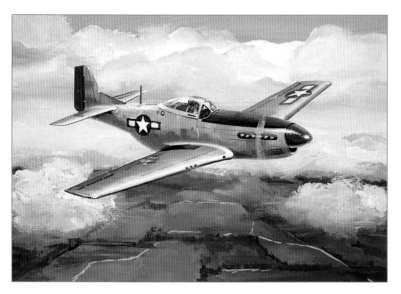

These paintings of two famous World War II fighters, a Mustang and a Spitfire, illustrate the ways in which light and shadows impact on the curved *airfoils*. An artist needs to note the wings and the horizontal stabilizers. ©*Andy Whyte, ASAA*

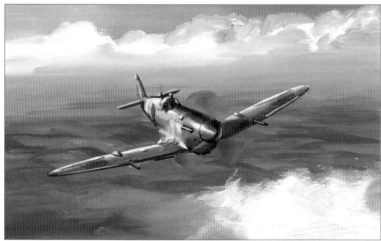

Pitch, the axis of flight that acts to move the aircraft up (to climb) and down (to dive), is controlled by the airplane's *elevator,* shown in orange. Moving the control stick back raises the elevators and causes the tail to move down, thus raising the nose to climb. Moving the control stick forward has the opposite effect and results in a dive. ©*Andy Whyte, ASAA*

PITCH, the first of the three, is the upward- or downward-acting movement that enables an aircraft to climb or to descend. It is controlled by the use of stabilators or elevators that are connected to the yoke or control stick in the pilot's hand.

ROLL, the second axis, is the turning or banking movement around the longitudinal axis—an imaginary line that extends from the nose of the craft through the aircraft's center of gravity (CG) and through the tail. Roll is controlled by ailerons that are also connected to the control yoke in the pilot's hand.

Moving the yoke or the stick to the right initiates a right turn. An artist should know that the aileron deflection is generally neutralized after the turn is established or the desired bank is achieved. A pilot

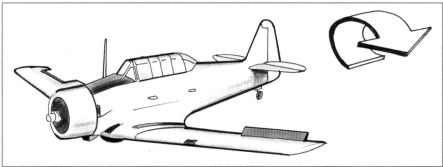

▲ *Roll, controlled by the* ailerons, *is the axis of flight that acts to bank and, therefore, to turn the aircraft. Shown in orange, the ailerons move in opposite directions under the control of the pilot's stick. As shown, the left aileron is up. This moves the left wing down and initiates a turn to the left.* ©Andy Whyte, ASAA

applies opposite aileron, in this case left aileron, to return to straight-and-level flight once the desired turn has been completed.

YAW, the third axis, is controlled, in most airplanes, by foot pedals that are connected to the rudder, a hinged control surface on the vertical stabilizer of the craft. Yaw acts around an imaginary line—the vertical axis—that extends from the top of the craft through the CG and out the bottom of the craft.

In your drawing, the position of the control surfaces should be in accord with the maneuver depicted in the painting.

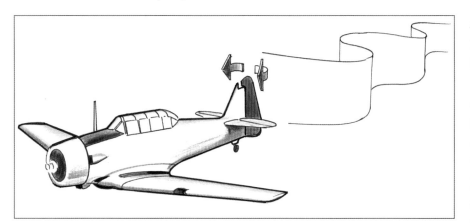

▲ *Yaw, the third flight axis, acts to move the airplane's nose from side to side and is controlled by the aircraft's* rudder, *the vertical surface shown in orange. The rudder is generally controlled by foot pedals in the cockpit. Pilots use the rudder to maintain alignment of the airplane with the direction of flight. An artist should keep in mind that the position of the control surfaces should be in accordance with the maneuver depicted in the drawing.* ©Andy Whyte, ASAA

AIRCRAFT DESIGN—FROM THE WRIGHT BROTHERS TO THE RAPTOR

Although man's search for mastery of flight began initially in balloons and gliders, the world celebrates the famous Wright Brothers' flights of December 17, 1903 as the first sustained, powered, and controlled flights. Until then, mankind had no bird's-eye view of the earth and the sky. In addition to a new perspective of land, water, and sky, the first flight unleashed an ongoing search in aircraft design. Design answers the question, "What is the aircraft's use?"

Aeronautical design engineering is a precise and highly complex subject. The process for creating a new aircraft to meet the buyer's requirements requires a detailed understanding of four interrelated and interdependent topics: Aerodynamics, Propulsion, Structures and Materials, and Manufacturing capability. Because there are some inherent limitations in each, the engineer's design work requires a series of progressive compromises—tradeoffs—to meet the client's requested specifications within budgetary constraints. Famed aircraft designer Igor Sikorsky said, "In the early days of aviation, the aircraft designers were also the test pilots. This had the automatic effect of weeding out the bad designers."

An aviation artist, in mastering his or her craft, will better depict the subject if there is understanding of designers' problems and solutions. To a large extent, accuracy in aviation art may be one key to a successful artistic career.

HOW AIRCRAFT DIFFER

Balloons

The earliest of flying machines, dating to the Montgolfier Brothers' ascent in 1783, hot-air balloons continue to delight huge numbers of people. Crowds gather for such festivals as that held annually in Albuquerque, New Mexico, where vivid colors and uniquely shaped balloons fill the skies against the rugged backdrop of the beautiful Sandia Mountains. The air, heated by the flames from burners controlled by the pilot, is lighter than surrounding ambient air and causes the balloon to rise. Air is expelled manually in order to descend. Balloons are propelled by air streams, and astute balloonists seek the flow of air at varying altitudes to obtain directional control of their craft.

Recently, a team of enthusiasts in Australia built a balloon, using three-fourths of a *mile* of aluminum-coated polyester film, 16 strips for each gore. Using two *miles* of tape, they laid the strips along a school hallway to tape them, adding 32 tether points. Sixteen gores were joined and taped. The cap, designed to be pulled downward to empty the balloon after flight, was 18 feet in diameter and was attached last.

Thanks to advances in science and technology, we can move between the home-built—as were all of the earliest pioneering aircraft—to the record-shattering. On March 20, 1999, Bertrand Piccard and Brian Jones circumnavigated the earth in their Breitling Orbiter. In 19 days, 1 hour, and 49 minutes, they became the first aviators to circle the globe nonstop in a hot-air balloon.

Airships

In the 1920s and 1930s, blimps and dirigibles were widely used for carrying passengers and for military purposes. The tragic crash and explosion of the hydrogen-laden *Hindenberg* at the conclusion of a trans-Atlantic flight brought on a hiatus in the use of airships. More recently, Goodyear blimps have been widely used in the United States and in Europe. Built for the purpose of drawing attention and advertising, blimps often carry television cameras to cover a variety of newsworthy events. With a swiveling single-wheel undercarriage, and two engines that can tilt to assist in take-off power, the Goodyear blimp is primarily a giant gasbag filled with helium. Because the hull must be kept under pressure, air-filled ballonets transfer pressure to the helium without mixing air with the helium.

In Germany, new lighter-than-air ships, CargoLifters, are due to start appearing in 2002. Designed to carry up to 160 tons, CargoLifters are another example of an aircraft design that is seeing a resurgence of interest made possible by great improvements in science and technology. The gasbags are airtight, multilayered films that reduce helium loss and are tougher, flame-resistant, more long-lasting, and lighter than fabrics used in the airships of the 1920s and 1930s.

Quote

"In the early days of aviation, the aircraft designers were also the test pilots. This had the automatic effect of weeding out the bad designers." *Igor Sikorsky*

Mastering Aerial Perspective

*Robert McCall,
ASAA Founder*

A premier aerospace artist, Robert McCall is imbued with a sense of wonder. "It isn't a calculated thing," he said. "I just am. In capturing the feelings that I have, I am trying to communicate my sense of awe about this wonderful, magical universe in which we live."

Despite the reality of the multinational space station, outer space exploration still seems futur-

The Spirit of NASA, **the merging of reality and illusion in Robert McCall's mural at Florida's EPCOT Center. ©Robert McCall, ASAA**

istic. Interestingly, the United States' exploration is rooted in almost a half-century of historical fact. McCall grounds his fantastic and imaginative visions in solid technological invention. Having studied scientific data that has been compiled over the past, McCall has researched space history as it was being created. Having witnessed the launch of the Thor-Able moon rocket at Cape Canaveral in 1957, McCall was present in NASA Mission Control for a landing on the moon and he manipulated the lunar rover camera in real time. He witnessed the test flights of the *Enterprise*, has worn the bulky space suits of U.S. space pioneers, and has flown the simulator in Houston with John Young, the commander of the first shuttle mission. In an article from the Smithsonian's *Air and Space* magazine, he has been called, "the man from the future," yet his imaginative vision is deeply rooted in the past.

McCall wrote, "In the 1930s, even the most optimistic did not dream that mankind would ever travel in space. Today, following three decades of incredible achievement, humanity is on the threshold of a new era in space exploration. . . . The wonderful possibilities are endless, as endless as the infinite regions that surround planet Earth."

In addition to having researched and witnessed the tools, machines, and theories of space exploration, it has been essential that Robert McCall develop a mastery of aerial perspective for his paintings that capture vast distances. His is the mastery of spatial depths, incredible light sources, reflective light, and dramatic intensities.

Helicopters

Stemming from the highly imaginative drawings of the fifteenth century genius Leonardo da Vinci, serious experimentations into helicopters began in earnest early in the 1900s. After having attempted an earlier model, aeronautical genius Igor Sikorsky flew his first practical single-rotor craft in 1939. The helicopter is a heavier-than-air craft that derives lift from a power-driven rotor or rotors that revolve horizontally on a vertical axis.

Since its introduction, the helicopter has been used for a variety of purposes, many of them in highly dramatic situations facing both the military and civilian communities. From clandestine combat operations to air-sea rescue and the movement of combat troops and outsized cargo, a variety of helicopter designs has become a mainstay of military and naval operations. Two Sikorsky HH-3Es performed the first non-stop helicopter crossing of the Atlantic Ocean, with the aid of nine aerial refuelings, in June 1967. This historic flight clearly demonstrated the capability of the modern helicopter.

In a variety of civilian roles, helicopter crew members fight forest fires, transport critically injured people to hospitals, chase criminals, report on traffic conditions, cover developing news events, and carry passengers on intracity routes. The helicopter's versatility seems endless and is a great source of dramatic drawings.

Gliders

Although there were many, like the Waco CG series that was used extensively during the World War II D-Day invasion of France, gliders today are most often beautiful sport craft that are flown solo or in dual flight. Gliding or soaring craft have the long wingspan that enables them to create lift using the natural wind and thermal activity. They rise on thermal columns of warm air, use the lift of wind flowing upward along mountain ridges, or use the wave lift that occurs when strong winds that are perpendicular to the mountains are deflected upward. In the latter, great altitude heights can be achieved. The world record is more than 49,000 feet.

For those who don't want to rely upon being towed aloft or on crew members required to assist in the launch, there are self-launching motor gliders. Some have foldaway engines that can be retracted into the glider once airborne.

Space Shuttle

Designed as a reusable vehicle for the exploration of outer space under the auspices of NASA, the National Aeronautics and Space Administration, a space shuttle is referred to as an Orbiter Vehicle. The space shuttle *Discovery* is OV-103. On October 11, 2000, with an empty weight of 151,419 pounds at rollout and 171,000 pounds with main engines installed, its mission was the continuing construction of the $60 billion International Space Station.

Discovery was the third of the orbiters to become operational at Florida's Kennedy Space Center. The first space shuttle mission was launched in 1981 and there have been many in the intervening years. The space shuttle blasts off vertically as a rocket and lands horizontally as a glider. With a pressurized crew compartment for up to seven, the orbiter has a large cargo bay upon which is mounted a remote

Quote

"Accuracy in aviation art may be one key to a successful artistic career."

25

manipulator system—a robot arm and hand with three joints analogous to the human shoulder, elbow, and wrist.

Solid rocket boosters provide most of the launch power, and much of the drama of launch, before they separate. The three main engines then continue to provide thrust until the shuttle reaches orbit. Orbital engines provide thrust for major changes in orbit and 44 small rocket engines are used for more exacting maneuvers. The largest single piece of the space shuttle is the external fuel tank that holds separate tanks of hydrogen fuel and oxygen oxidizer that power the shuttle's three main engines.

The space shuttle lands without power in a manner similar to an airplane "dead stick" landing or the landing of a glider or sailplane. Experimental craft—lifting bodies—were investigated in the late 1960s as potential space vehicles that could be used on a gliding descent from orbit. The entire undersurface of the craft has to function as a lifting surface and formed the design basis for the space shuttle—the ultimate glider.

AERODYNAMICS, MATERIALS, AND MANUFACTURING— LIMITING FACTORS OF AIRCRAFT DESIGN

In the design and building of aircraft there is nothing that is added that is not absolutely necessary. An aircraft designer deals with lift, weight, thrust, and drag and how they interrelate. A change in one affects the others.

Lift can be increased temporarily through the use of high-lift devices: flaps, slots, and/or slats, which complement each other. However, the addition of the high-lift device–operating mechanisms causes an increase in weight, and any increase in lift results in an increase in drag. In extending the flaps, lift is increased. By adding slots or slats to the flap-equipped wing, a further increase in lift occurs. Recognizing these devices, when they are used and why, will enhance the accuracy of your drawings.

When lift is created, upward swirls of air at the tip of each wing, known as wingtip vortices, are also created. The swirls of air flow from the higher pressure beneath the airfoils to the area of lower pressure above the airfoils. To counteract wingtip vortices and their ability to affect the ailerons, designers shortened the length of the ailerons. They also placed functional devices, such as fuel tanks, armaments, and winglets, at the wing

⬇ Temporary increases in *lift* can be achieved through the use of *flaps* and *slots,* which can be movable or fixed. The added weight of the devices necessary to move flaps and slots represents another tradeoff. Recognizing the degree of flap and slot settings is important to the artist. ©*Andy Whyte, ASAA*

Flaps  30 degrees

 10 degrees

Increase drag for landing

Increase lift for take off and maneuvers

Slots

Movable slots

Fixed slot

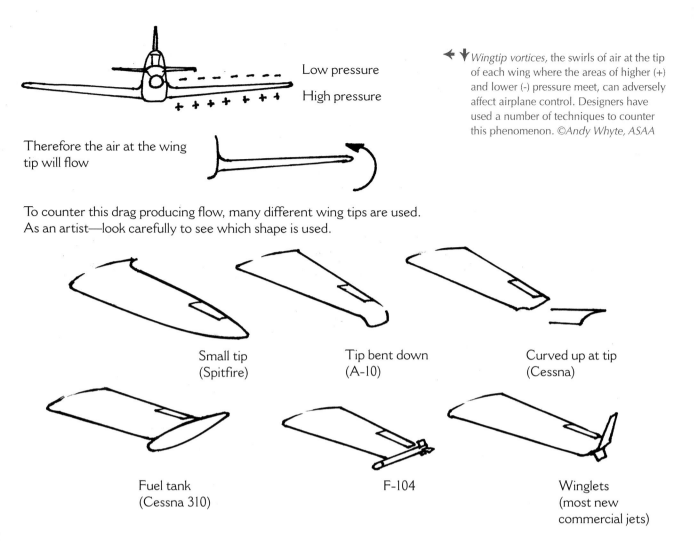

Low pressure

High pressure

Therefore the air at the wing tip will flow

To counter this drag producing flow, many different wing tips are used. As an artist—look carefully to see which shape is used.

Small tip
(Spitfire)

Tip bent down
(A-10)

Curved up at tip
(Cessna)

Fuel tank
(Cessna 310)

F-104

Winglets
(most new
commercial jets)

tips. On some commercial jet aircraft, winglets are 10 to 12 feet high. As with understanding the use and results of the major control surfaces—ailerons, elevators, and rudders—knowledge of the use, shape, and placement of the flaps, spoilers, winglets, and trim tabs will increase artistic accuracy.

Objects moving through the air create a turbulent flow of air—a boundary layer—around an airfoil. Air intakes, which work best with a smooth air flow, find this turbulence detrimental to performance. Therefore, the inlets for air intake to engines, oil coolers, and so forth, are separated from the fuselage or wings. Be aware of these separations when you are drawing aircraft, especially jets.

PROPULSION

Propulsion is the study of the power required to achieve the design objectives and the advantages and disadvantages of each engine type. An aircraft designer has to select the right propulsion system for each particular design and the goal is to achieve fuel efficiency, low engine weight to horsepower ratio, low total system weight, reliability, ease of maintenance, and noise reduction.

✈ ↓ Objects moving through the air create a turbulent *boundary layer* along their surfaces. This turbulence is detrimental to engines and oil coolers that need a smooth air intake to perform well. Designers have separated the intakes from the surfaces for this reason and artists need to be aware of these separations, especially with jet aircraft. The following drawings show some examples. (below)–P-51 Mustang; (middle right)–DC-3; (lower left)– DC-10; (lower right)–F-4 Phantom. ©Andy Whyte, ASAA

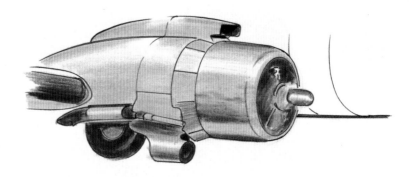

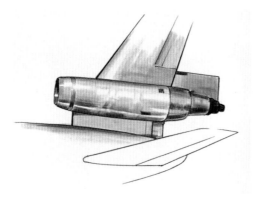

The Key to Success as an Artist? Hard Work and Discipline!

R. G. Smith, ASAA Founder

Curtiss Seagull
A Curtiss SOC-1 Seagull lands next to the USS *Mississippi* **during the 1930s.** ©*R. G. Smith, ASAA, Courtesy National Air & Space Museum Collection*

There are no secrets and no shortcuts to becoming a successful artist.

"Achievement comes from hard work, discipline, and a constant program of practice and learning," said R. G. Smith. "Aspiring artists want to know how to draw and paint, but very few want to take the time to learn. . . . The key to success is to refrain from ever being satisfied with your work. Never stop rehearsing your craft. Every painting is another step in an endless learning curve."

One of the luckiest days of his career was to meet an artist, Arthur Beaumont, who taught him composition, color balance, and how to translate his visual images to paper or canvas. The most valuable lesson, however, was discipline and to treat every painting as if it were a problem to be solved.

R. G. admitted, "The three key elements in my approach to painting were: accuracy, planning, and the power of suggestion. Accuracy requires study and thorough knowledge of your subject. Generally, more than 50 percent of the time I invested in a painting went into research."

R. G. started collecting research material—photographs, drawings, articles that profiled aircraft, pictures of clouds, and paint chips or samples from aircraft for color accuracy. He planned his paintings by making several sketches of ideas before deciding on a final composition.

He suggested: "Create the background first, knowing beforehand where you intend to place the aircraft, which should be the last phase of your painting. It often took me three or four days just to put a background together. . . . I liked to put an airplane *in* a picture, not *on* it.

Two Navy TA-4J aircraft. As a design engineer for McDonnell Douglas, R. G. made major contributions to this aircraft. ©*R. G. Smith, ASAA*

"Learn how to use the power of suggestion," R. G. said. "I try to convey a sense of reality, atmosphere, and energy. I am usually more scientific than theoretical. Yet, if you examine my paintings up close, you will note that much of my brushwork is rather loose. Stand back and you will see that the overall effect is somewhat like a photograph. It has long been my theory that the eye and the brain do most of the work. . . . In other words, you don't have to include every detail, just a suggestion of detail."

As an aeronautical engineer, R. G. had a distinct advantage in his knowledge and thorough understanding of the construction and function of an airplane. "This applies," he said, "to any subject matter. If you want to draw figures or nudes, learn the structure of the human body first. . . . I am convinced that if you gain knowledge of the inner workings of your subject, you can literally give it life."

He also suggested the study of the works of artists you admire or whose style you want to emulate. If you want to paint ocean scenes, study those who are successful at marine art and the elements of water and weather.

R. G., one of the outstanding aviation artists whose style and incredible talent you might want to emulate, said, "There are a couple of clichés that apply to painting and I ascribe to both. 'Build your stage and put the actors in it,' and 'Put the subject matter in the picture, not on it.'

"Some artists only see airplanes as mechanical objects. As a result, their depictions of them become mechanical, stilted portraits rather than a picture with character, motion, or some measure of dramatic quality.

◀▼ Supermarine Spitfire with an
inline engine.

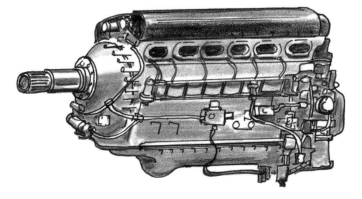

▲▶ Grumman F8F Bearcat with a radial
engine. Prior to the widespread
introduction of jet engines, airplane
designers relied on two main types of
reciprocating or piston engines—the
inline, shown on the Spitfire, and the
radial, shown on the Bearcat. Each type
had advantages and disadvantages.
©Andy Whyte, ASAA

The earliest forms of propulsion were simple, low-horsepower piston engines that turned propellers. There are two main types of piston engines —the radial and the inline. This refers to the placement of the cylinders in relation to each other. Each design has its merits and its deficiencies. The radial has higher drag, but it is a more compact unit, requires shorter engine mounts, and is less susceptible to battle damage. The inline has less drag, but requires a radiator for cooling and longer engine mounts.

More powerful and mechanically simpler, jet engines were first used during World War II and entered service on commercial airliners in the 1950s. A jet takes in air, compresses it through a series of compressor blades, mixes fuel with the hot, compressed air, and ignites the mixture in a combustion chamber. The resulting explosion of hot gas from the rear of the engine creates thrust, *pushing* the aircraft forward. The hot gas also simultaneously turns a turbine wheel that is connected by a center shaft to the compressor blades and keeps the compressor blades spinning.

The three basic types of jet engines are turbojets, turbofans or fanjets, and turboprops or propjets. The turbojets use exhaust thrust to propel the aircraft. Turbofans or fanjets have a larger fan at the front. While they take in more air, they divert some of the air around the combustion chamber and later mix it with hot exhaust gases escaping out the back. This lowers the temperature and speed of the exhaust and results in a quieter engine.

In the 50 years since World War II, there have been many great leaps forward in aircraft design, in the materials used, and in manufacturing capabilities. Many of these advances have had their beginnings in the space program. Supersonic flight is an everyday occurrence, man has walked on the moon, and the International Space Station is a reality. Spacecraft, airplane, helicopter, dirigible, and blimp design has kept pace, and new capabilities are enabling improved mission performance. Acquaint yourself fully with the design of the aircraft that you are drawing and practice drawing exacting portions of the craft as avidly as did the design engineer who originally created it.

Knowing basic aerodynamics and its influence on the design of aircraft helps an aviation artist capture the history, beauty, and functionality of the craft being depicted. Keeping pace with its continual evolution is not only intriguing, it is an inspiration to further drawing and painting.

Quote

"Never stop rehearsing your craft. Every painting is another step in an endless learning curve."
R.G. Smith, ASAA Founder

↑ *Turbojet* engines, shown in this drawing, often power high-speed fighter aircraft like this F-104. They are reliable and have evolved to higher thrust/weight ratios and overall smaller size. ©*Andy Whyte, ASAA*

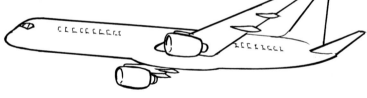

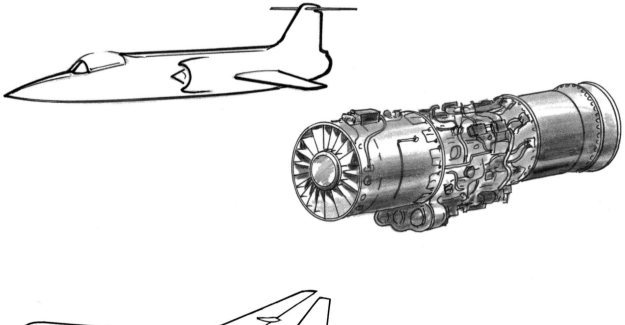

↑→ *Turbofan* engines—fanjets—power many modern airliners like the B-757. They take in more air and operate more quietly. Their shape is distinctive. ©*Andy Whyte, ASAA*

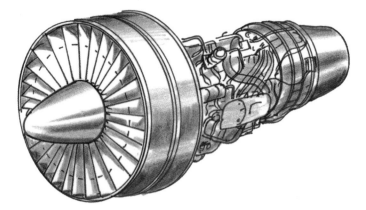

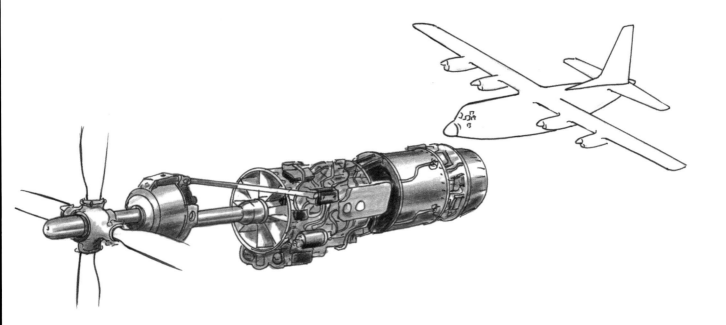

▲ *Turboprop* engines have found wide use on short-range commercial aircraft and on military cargo carriers like the Lockheed C-130 Hercules. Also highly reliable, they combine the propeller's thrust with that of the jet's exhaust gases. ©*Andy Whyte, ASAA*

"With a pencil, you can create perspective, light, and shade. You can create a three-dimensional look by using different weight to the penciled lines." *Andy Whyte, ASAA*

THE TOOLS OF THE TRADE:

To Start, You Need a Pencil and Paper

➤ The variety of pencils and papers that are available to the artist is almost overwhelming. Colored pencils, Prismacolor, sketching pencils, graphite pencils and sticks, and carbon pencils and sticks are some possible choices for the artist. Start simply and, as your drawing improves, experiment with different surfaces and techniques by trying the wide range of erasers, sketch pads, and papers offered.

Today's artists are provided with a huge selection of drawing boards, drawing paper, drawing instruments, and painting supplies. More advanced artists settle on their preferred tools and drawing methods through time and practice; a beginner needs many questions answered before getting started in drawing. Sure, a pencil and paper are all you really need. But, *"Which* pencil and *which* paper?"

To draw requires developing a successful eye-to-hand coordination and the ability to draw what your eye or your mind's eye sees. Although you may look forward eagerly to using paints and color, first concentrate on learning to draw and on light, shade, and value. As a pilot considers a good landing to be the result of a good approach, a good drawing is the result of having properly developed the basics.

Start with pencil and paper. Start modestly and work your way to the materials that fit your increasing ability and developing style.

PENCILS

Pencil manufacturers use a ratio of graphite to clay in creating pencil lead; the more graphite, the blacker and softer the grade of pencil. Hardness is designated by letter, i.e., softer leads are titled B for black and harder leads are titled H, combined with a number. This results in designating pencils from 9H (the hardest), through 8H, to 2H, H, F, HB, B, 2B through 8B, to 9B (the softest). Part of the fun in choosing a combination of pencils and paper is that the experimentation itself can add variety to your beginning practice in drawing. Start out with pencils graded from 2H through 2B for sketching.

For shading and tonal values, some artists prefer crosshatching—making firm, rapid, and strong, sharply defined lines that give form, shape, and value throughout a picture. Using a 2B lead that is conducive to shading and blending, tonal values also can be achieved through blurring, smoothing, or defining the penciled strokes with a combination of the use of erasers and/or tightly wound paper spirals called stumps or tortillions.

PAPER, BOARDS, AND SKETCHPADS

Before you leap into the world of painting, first learn to DRAW! You may soon begin a search for canvas and wood and Masonite surfaces on which to work (see chapter 13), but we urge that you start at the beginning. Practice drawing and choose the best surfaces for drawing and sketching: paper, boards, and sketchpads.

Cartridge paper is named for the use to which it was originally put—as packaging paper for holding a charge of powder in a weapon. The name has lasted. Cartridge paper is used for pencil drawings and also for charcoal. This acid-free paper is more reliable for permanence and is available in pads as well as in single sheets.

When selecting a board, choose one with an alkaline buffering or one that is acid-free or has a substrate that uses a starch-based, acid-free adhesive. Hard-surfaced papers offer a smooth, dense surface upon which to draw.

For variety, try vellum, oil painting paper, and Ingres paper, which lends itself well to pastels, pencils, and crayons, and give texture for a variety of techniques. Try charcoal and pastel paper in a variety of colors or watercolor paper that can be rough or smooth. Handmade papers and pure linen, calligraphy, and blotting papers might interest you and challenge your techniques.

For layout and compositional work, tracing and graph papers are useful. You will want a supply of masking tape or drafting tape for securing paper to your drawing surface.

CHARCOAL

Charcoal is a form of carbon that is created by partially burning or oxidizing wood, generally willow. Available in its natural form, natural charcoal sticks can be messy for an artist's use; some varieties of sticks are wrapped in peel-off paper covers for ease of use. Spray fixatives can help to control the dust. Artists' charcoal is also available as powder or

▲ You don't need to purchase everything on the market. To do charcoal drawings and pen-and-inks, buy a few and experiment with as wide a variety as your drawings require. A wide range of papers, pens, and inks are offered; practice helps with making the right choices.

Painting with an Airbrush

Chad S. Bailey

Though considered a modern tool, the airbrush can trace its origins from the prehistoric caves at Lascaux, near Montignac, in the Dordogne region of France. Prehistoric man ground chunks of red and yellow ocher into powder and painted on walls using his hands as stencils. From these early beginnings the airbrush, an atomizer using compressed air to spray paint, has developed into a unique and useful tool.

Using masks, stencils, or free hand to direct the paint and to prevent overspray on the surface of the painting, an airbrush can deliver color from the width of a fine line to a wide spray pattern. There are different types of airbrushes and a variety of airbrush manufacturers. Airbrushes come in a wide range of prices and capabilities. Some mix the paint and air internally inside the head. Some have a gravity system and some a siphon system. Choose the airbrush that best meets your needs. You have a wide choice!

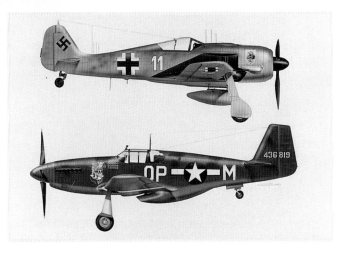

Focke-Wulf 190 and a North American P-51 Mustang. *©Chad Bailey*

Internal mix airbrushes, which combine the air and paint in the head assembly, produce a thoroughly atomized fine dot spray. In an airbrush that mixes the air and paint externally, the spray pattern is composed of larger dots. An airbrush with a trigger that controls only the flow of air is considered to be single action and the paint spray is regulated by an adjustment screw (in an internal mix airbrush) or by twisting the fluid cap on the paint tip (in the external mix).

Airbrushes with triggers that control the air *and* the color are considered to be dual action. These let you change line width, values, and paint opacity while the hand is in motion. Chad Bailey, Artist Member of ASAA, paints with pigments and brushes and also paints with an airbrush. In Bailey's opinion, the dual action airbrushes offer finer control. He said, "Though they may be more expensive, they are worth the price."

In an airbrush with gravity feed, color cups are mounted above the head assembly and the paint moves downward in reaction to the pull of gravity. A gravity feed requires less air pressure and gives you an opportunity to use slower hand movement for better detail. Bailey added, "It also allows for quick paint changes, believe it or not, because it is easier to clean the cup."

F-15 Eagle. *©Chad Bailey*

When the color cup is connected below the head assembly, the paint is siphoned to the assembly. In the siphon feed system, a variety of color cups can be accessed and colors can be changed more quickly and easily. Experienced with airbrush techniques, Bailey has a preference for Iwata Airbrushes. He calls them the "finest in the world."

A third variety, the side feed airbrush, has a small color cup fitted onto the side. This allows you to rotate the assembly and to work on horizontal or vertical surfaces.

"The process of painting with an airbrush is as varied as there are artists," said Bailey. "An airbrush siphons paint from a reservoir using air pressure, then atomizes the paint into small particles that stick to the surface of the canvas. Mixing paint in the reservoir can produce variations of color, or this may also be done directly on the surface of the canvas. This is very similar to the way printing is done by placing dots of pigment close to each other and allowing the human eye to do the mixing."

A glaze, which can be rendered by spraying a pigment reduced with water, creates the illusion of depth when applied in multiple layers. By using red, yellow, or orange, an artist can "warm" up different parts of the painting by glazing. Conversely, by using green, blue, or purple, a "cooling" down can be achieved. As with any tool, the airbrush has its limitations and is only as good as the talent of the artist who wields it.

in compressed sticks or pencils. The compressed forms range in grades, can be purchased in thick, medium, and thin widths, and the compressed pencils are available in soft, medium, and hard. Charcoal can lend itself to dark shades, can be easily blended with your finger or with a stump, and highlights can be picked up with an eraser.

PENS AND MARKERS

A wide variety of pens also exists. Use inks that will not fade when exposed to sunlight and experiment with dip and reservoir pens. Dip pens, the most basic, are easy to use. Brush pens come in single, double, and five line forms. Fiber and felt-tip pens give dense black lines. Fine fiber-tipped pens respond well to rapid sketching and have the added strength of a tip supported by a metal sleeve. Some pens are useful for thumbnail sketches and allow an artist to quickly establish tonal and linear compositions with a minimum of detail (see chapter 11).

Felt-tipped markers, which come in an array of colors, are alcohol- and chemical-based. The alcohol-based are safer for your health.

Charcoal, pens, and markers can allow you to develop a different style of artwork, but can be more challenging than pencil in that they cannot be erased. On the other hand, this experimentation can lead to greater eye-to-hand coordination.

STARTING A STUDIO

Don't let the lack of a studio hold you back. You can draw outside. You can draw in a limited space. Sure, in the best of art worlds, your own studio is desired. If you should be so lucky, equip it with a large surface upon which to draw and with adequate room for your miscellaneous aids—sketches, photographs, and reference material. Plan for a good source of natural light, preferably north light, and good overhead lighting.

Handy additions to your studio are a spray fixative (simply an over-the-counter hair spray, for starters) for pastel, charcoal, and pencil drawings and a solvent or thinner that will act as a cleanser for equipment. You'll want to have your choice of methods of sharpening pencils and a supply of erasers—putty rubber, white erasers that fit the palm of the hand, kneaded erasers, and/or slices of ordinary rubber eraser that are trimmed to a chisel shape for erasing in a thin line. That edge, when dirtied, can be shaved for reuse with another piece of useful equipment—a sharp craft knife. A large, soft watercolor wash brush can be used to disperse eraser debris.

For circles, ellipses, and curved surfaces, you may want to obtain sets of stencil templates and sweeps. T-squares, straight-edges, and French curves can be added to your toolbox as the needs arise. Use these as aids and not as substitutes for the practice of freehand drawing. To learn to draw, you have to draw, draw, and draw some more.

↟ Art supply stores carry hundreds of different color markers—fiber and felt-tip markers come in all colors with tips of varying widths. From a health standpoint, the alcohol-based marker ink is preferred. Marker paper is available in all sizes for sketching quickly as well as for finished drawings.

↟ Artist supplies for painting—brushes, palette knives, palettes, pigments and paints, and an extensive array of accessories—are discussed in chapter 12. Through practice and experimentation with all of the drawing tools available in well-equipped art supply stores, your curiosity will lead to similar practice and experimentation with the tools used for painting.

An airbrush—an atomizer that uses compressed air as the propellant for spraying paint—is another useful tool for aviation art. Choose the one that best accomplishes your needs. You have a choice!

COMPUTERS

Like a pencil, the computer is a tool. Undeniably, art has been affected greatly by the use of the computer; many sculptors, filmmakers, architects, and other visual artists use computers. However, a computer won't make a better artist out of you. As with launching into painting, before you experiment too heavily with some of the software that is available, be certain that you've spent time learning to draw. Computer programs can diversify your drawing pleasure, but they are no substitute for developing your own talent.

Programs that are available include, to name a few, Adobe Illustrator and Adobe Photoshop, CorelDraw, Deneba's Canvas, Macromedia FreeHand, and Jasc Paint Shop Pro. These software programs are designed to assist an artist in creating and producing illustrations and designs for printing and for use on the Web. They include photo manipulation and can help you to develop graphics from line art to animation. You can add a flatbed scanner to your computer system, scan your own drawing into one of these programs, and develop the design further. You could add a digital pressure-sensitive pad and stylus to your computer and hand-sketch your drawing to the drawing software for further manipulation.

The use of computers can help to develop your eye and your eye-to-hand coordination. The computer can be a useful tool, but it is just that—a tool. The final word will still be, "Learn to draw!"

From a Sketch to a Computer Generation
John Sarsfield

John Sarsfield enjoys looking downward upon flying aircraft. In this view, he directly faces and accepts the challenge of creating the atmospheric perspective that is so essential to aviation art and to simultaneously give a sense of motion to each craft. Generally, Sarsfield banks or places his aircraft on a slight diagonal to indicate action and he includes his aircraft as integral and important *to* the scene as well as placing them *in* the scene.

Sarsfield researches carefully to select landscapes that are even more intriguing when seen from above. His viewers are given the chance to become airborne themselves, as if flying in a craft at a higher altitude, flying in formation and in a chase position, or being drawn into the scene with a bird's-eye view and given the feeling of greater heights and more vast distances. He said, "My usual practice is to work with small, crude thumbnails until the general idea of the composition appeals to me. I follow that with a computer-generated outline. That outline is fleshed out directly on the painting after I complete the background."

Sarsfield created his own computer program, entering the aircraft with the use of illustration software. When operating his program, a craft is selected and will appear on the monitor in the side view. By clicking on the numbers at the bottom of his screen, he can move the craft through the yaw and roll axes and select views that best enhance his compositions. His computer program doesn't create the drawing. In a very real sense, he is using the computer as a tool that aids his drawing and the composing of his scenes.

Sarsfield painting of a bright yellow Piper Cub above the mill was simply, 'a pretty picture of a popular airplane.' From nine thumbnails of rough conceptual sketches that included the two items of interest, the mill and the Piper Cub, Sarsfield made compositional choices. As shown, his resulting computer generated drawing depicts a 78-foot distance from the viewer, a minus 146° yaw and a 5° roll to the left. ©*John Sarsfield*

Learning Never Stops

Jim Laurier, ASAA

Having drawn airplanes since he could hold a pencil, Jim Laurier admitted that attaining his pilot certificate was "the icing on the cake." In pursuing his art career, Laurier has flown in a variety of aircraft including a P-51 Mustang, hot-air balloon, helicopter, and an assortment of light aircraft. Although he can and does draw and paint many different things, aviation remains his favorite subject.

An honors graduate of the Paier School of Art in Connecticut, Laurier began as a freelance illustrator in New York City and, on his first assignment, illustrated a book jacket for a story about a B-25 bomber crew fighting in World War II in the Solomon Islands. Having developed a reputation for high quality, Laurier combines technical accuracy with a realistic portrayal of aircraft in action and draws his viewers into his scenes.

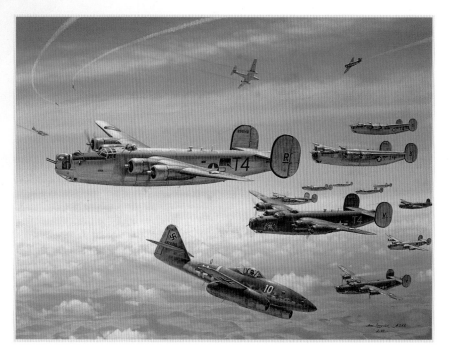

R Bar over Bielefeld
On November 2, 1944, B-24 bombers of the 489th Bomb Group were sent to destroy the railroad marshalling yards at Bielefeld, Germany. In one of the earliest attacks against U.S. heavy bombers by jet aircraft, the bomber crews were surprised by their first encounter with the new German jet fighters, Messerschmitt Me-262s. The German jets were chased off by P-47s of the 56th Fighter Group that were escorting the bombers that day. There were no losses on either side. ©*James Laurier, ASAA*

Laurier uses his computer to help in the creation of his art. He said, "My method of madness is to use Adobe Photoshop for many finished book illustrations and often for manipulating my sketches for paintings."

He takes several different approaches. He sometimes scans his thumbnail sketches to resize, rearrange, redraw, and/or refine his original line drawings. He added, "Sometimes, I scan several separate drawings and compose a final composition on the computer. At this point I may leave the image as a line drawing or I may make it a grayscale image by adding in shaded areas to work out my value patterns and lighting scheme. I may also go all the way to a full-color comp to work out all the problems before the painting."

Laurier may also make two versions of his sketch—one a line drawing and one a grayscale or color image. He uses the printout of the line drawing to transfer the image to canvas as, he said, "The line art is easier to work with for this purpose. I print out my images and take them to a service bureau to have them enlarged to the actual size of my painting. In most cases, I've made drawing refinements on my large-scale printout. Laying the enlarged printout over my canvas, and with a large piece of my homemade carbon paper underneath, I trace the image onto the canvas.

"Usually, my digital sketches are 'low-res' (low resolution) (72 dpi to 150 dpi). With the finished illustration for a book, I first find out the line screen that the printing press will be running and I make my image resolution higher, usually 340 dpi. This has to be determined before beginning the illustration."

Although Laurier would be the first to say that the computer is simply another tool, no substitute for learning to draw, he joins a growing number of those who continue to learn how to best utilize this technological tool. He said, "The computer is a real time saver. The ability to experiment with sketches reveals possibilities that otherwise may have been overlooked."

f you watch an aircraft fly past, the craft is fairly detailed and sharp and the background is blurred. That is because your eyes are focused on the aircraft." *Andy Whyte, ASAA*

CONSIDERATIONS IN DRAWING AIRCRAFT

Know Your Subject—From the Ground up

Drawing aircraft and spacecraft introduces unique problems. There can be major differences between an aircraft that is idle on the ground and that same craft when airborne. For your drawings, beware of relying too heavily on photographs and on model aircraft when you choose a particular view. Errors are made if a craft photographed on the ground is transposed into a drawing of the craft flying and, conversely, when a photograph of a flying craft is drawn as if it is parked on the ground. Know your subject! Do your homework!

MAJOR DIFFERENCES BETWEEN IDLE AND FLYING AIRCRAFT

Aerodynamic changes take place as an aircraft takes to the air. All aircraft will have differences in wing position from the static position to flight, although it is less noticeable on aircraft with shorter wingspans. A long-winged B-52 bomber, fully fueled and parked on the ramp, will have wings bent downward with the pull of gravity, their weight supported with outrigger landing gear. The wings bear their structural weight and the weight of the loaded fuel tanks and four engines. The tires and the landing gear struts are depressed.

The same craft, once airborne, will have dropped the outrigger wheels and will display wings that rise with the lift that carries the craft upward. All wings have to flex with their aerodynamic changes; in some aircraft that flex amounts to a matter of feet. Immediately after takeoff, the aircraft wingtips, though heavily loaded, will rise, the landing gear struts will extend, and the wheels, no longer bearing the

➜ The B-52 Stratofortress on the ramp shows the downward deflection of the wings with the weight of the structure, fuel, and engines. Note the landing gear and the landing gear door as well as interest created by the lighting and the cast shadows. Note, too, the diffused haze and the remaining puddles left from a recent rain. The buildings in the background keep the eye of the viewer moving throughout the drawing. ©*Andy Whyte, ASAA*

weight of the craft, will be rounded ellipses, still spinning with the roll of the takeoff. Then the gear will start rotating through retraction.

KNOW DIFFERENCES IN LANDING GEAR CONFIGURATION

Upon landing, there are dramatic differences in landing gear as well. The landing gear consists of wheels, tires, brakes, shock absorbers, axles, and other support structure. Know whether the subject aircraft has main gear and a tail wheel—is a "taildragger"—or whether it has main gear and a nose wheel. Most commercial jet aircraft, for example, have nose wheels with two tires and have two or more main gear assemblies with as many as 16 tires.

Know whether the gear is fixed, whether it retracts, and, if so, *how* it retracts. Know the design configuration of the subject craft. How is the gear stowed in the belly of the Cessna 210? When cycled, it appears to elongate directly below the craft, each gear leg rotating inwardly before both slide into the fuselage below the cabin. Some aircraft have gear doors affixed directly to the struts; some wheels disappear completely into wheel wells beneath the pilot position and have separate gear doors that close after the wheels are up and locked; some are not covered; and some wheels, when retracted, still extend below the lower curvature of the wing.

USE PHOTOGRAPHS AND MODEL AIRCRAFT AS TOOLS

Photos and models are valuable tools, but know their limitations. Don't depend upon one photograph of an aircraft to show these dramatic changes and don't depend upon a model of the aircraft to show the dynamics of flight. If you photograph your subject aircraft, which is on display at your favorite museum, beware of using the photo as a sole reference for drawing the craft. The tire pressure alone can throw the drawing off. What weight difference exists between the museum craft and the fully loaded combat-ready warplane, and how much more compressed are the tires of the heavier aircraft?

When using an aircraft model, consider it a secondary aid. Take the model outside in the sunlight conditions that you have chosen for your drawing. The model aircraft will help to define how shadows fall and what parts of the aircraft will be shadowed by others. It will help to define the best angle to highlight the craft for dramatic appeal. It will *not* show the flex in the wings, the retraction of the wheels—the action of flight.

Recognize that some ancillary equipment that is visible on the idle aircraft, e.g., *Remove Before Flight* streamers, pitot covers, control locks,

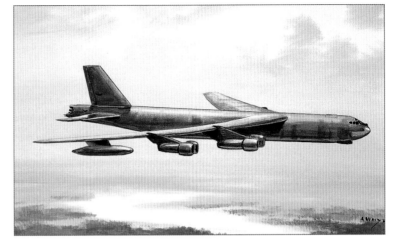

▲ The same B-52 Stratofortress has different characteristics when airborne. The wings flex and are deflected upward. The light and the shadows differ, too. Note the terrain, the winding river, and the horizon in the distance. ©*Andy Whyte, ASAA*

▲ The strut is fully extended and the tire fully rounded, as it would be just prior to touchdown. ©Andy Whyte, ASAA

▲ The strut is almost fully depressed and the tire flattened upon landing. Note the dust raised at impact. ©Andy Whyte, ASAA

▲ The landing gear during rollout or taxiing to parking shows some strut deflection and a slight flattening of the tire. ©Andy Whyte, ASAA

Demonstrating the changes in the configuration of the landing gear, the strut extension and the tire depression are major clues to the aircraft's position in respect to the ground.

air intake protectors, or chocks holding the wheels, cannot be included in a drawing of the craft in flight. Know and understand aircraft equipment and its uses. Including some equipment can enhance your drawing or it could be completely out of place in your scene.

OTHER DIFFERENCES UNIQUE TO AVIATION ART

What about depicting an aircraft that has just lost one of its propeller-driven engines? It is the artist's responsibility to understand aerodynamic factors. An aircraft that suddenly loses an engine has a tendency to yaw into the wing with the dead engine. The pilot pushes the opposite rudder pedal to full deflection to counteract the yaw, feathers (or flattens the pitch of) the prop on the dead engine to reduce drag, and maintains directional control by neutralizing any bank—maintaining a 0 degree of aileron deflection. In a sudden engine-out situation, even a slight amount of bank can result in a wicked and rapid snap of the aircraft into the wing the pilot is trying to lift. In discussing flying the B-24, Wilson Hurley noted that "even as little as a 10-degree deflection in the down aileron caused an abrupt separation of the airflow over the wing— an aileron stall. . . . If I were to show a B-24 with an outboard feathered, I'd paint opposite rudders fully deflected and ailerons flat."

In drawing the vortices of air that stream from a fighter aircraft like the F-16 during a high-G maneuver, it is important to know that the air spirals occur first at the strakes that are the juncture of the wing and the fuselage. There are also wingtip vortices that rotate inward toward the fuselage. Both depend upon the water vapor content and air temperature and condensation of that water vapor. If you include these vortices in your drawing, be sure that high humidity is possible—include puddles showing recent rain, a nearby waterfront or river, or moisture-laden clouds.

Aircraft have exhaust nozzles that can be controlled by the pilot's use of the throttle. Know some of the differences when drawing fighter jets. In an AV-8 Harrier, the downward vectoring of the exhaust thrust gives the unique capabilities of vertical takeoff, hover, and rotation in a horizontally stable position. Vectored thrust in an F-22 gives the heavy fighter nimble agility in turning flight. Some exhaust nozzles are shrouded and not visible, as on the A-7, the A-10, and the T-38. Some, as on the F-16, are externally visible. Most commonly in normal cruise the F-16 nozzle is tightly closed. When throttled back for a descent for a landing or taxiing and when the jet is thrust into afterburner, the nozzles are open.

Very little sensation of speed is seen or felt by the view from the cockpits of high-altitude jets at elevations that take them above most weather conditions. Indications of relative speed can be shown by a blurring of the exhaust gases. As aircraft fly closer to the earth, relative speed is much more obvious. Consider blurring the background when you depict an aircraft close to terrain.

KNOW SOME BASICS ABOUT WEATHER

To draw aircraft is to draw them in their element—the air. If you have not been flying, take a few flights with instructors from your local airport. Tune your senses to see, hear, and feel some of the sensations of flying. Get an appreciation for the major elements of the weather—temperature, pressure, and air masses—and some indications of certain weather conditions. Cloud types are specifically linked to atmospheric conditions, heights, and the pressure differential. Cumulus clouds—great background for dynamic aerial images—are indicative of instability, updrafts, turbulence, and, outside of the clouds, good visibility. Stratus clouds, indicating very little vertical movement, can be linked with haze, fog, and poor visibility. Stratus clouds can offer a calming image for your drawing.

Learn about weather that is hazardous to pilots—heavy winds, obscuring visibilities, hail, and the turbulent air that is found in thunderstorms. Most weather conditions occur in the troposphere that extends to an average of approximately 35,000 feet. Many commercial jets fly above these altitudes over our contiguous United States. General aviation aircraft are limited primarily to flight below those levels—*in* the weather conditions that can enhance flight or, in the case of adverse conditions, can be hazardous to the aircraft and to its occupants. Military aircraft that are designed to be all-weather craft still face limitations in the advent of extremely severe and violent storms. The renowned author Richard Bach said of painting his experience in a fighter jet in the midst of a vicious thunderstorm, "All you would need is six tubes of black paint."

▲ Andy Whyte's B-24 Liberator is depicted in hazardous weather, with two engines out on the right wing. The propellers are feathered to reduce drag, the ailerons are neutral, and the rudders are fully deflected to the left, the opposite side from the inoperative engines, in order to maintain directional control. Notice the reflection of the atmospheric coloration in the surfaces of the aircraft. ©Andy Whyte, ASAA

▼ The F-16 Fighting Falcon is streaking for takeoff at twilight with full afterburner engaged. The engine nozzle, which would be tightly closed in cruise configuration, is fully opened when the jet is in afterburner. ©Andy Whyte, ASAA

Telling the Story

Alex Durr

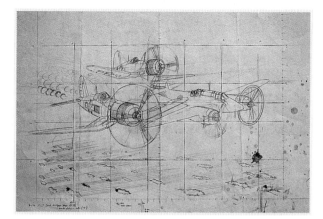

Having taken the island of Okinawa during World War II, U.S. naval forces anchored offshore took some devastating losses. After having been subjected daily to intense Japanese kamikaze bombing raids, they determined that the raids were guided by a lone high-altitude reconnaissance Kawasaki Ki-45 *Toryu* (Dragon Slayer), code-named "Nick" by the Allies. It appeared that an end to the kamikaze raids might be achieved were the "Nick" to be pursued and downed.

Alex Durr was commissioned to create a painting by a World War II pilot who had been part of the defensive response to the deadly attacks. Long after the war was over, Ken Reusser saw another of Durr's paintings about the air war in the Pacific. Reusser contacted Durr and requested that he paint *Kannibal Ken*.

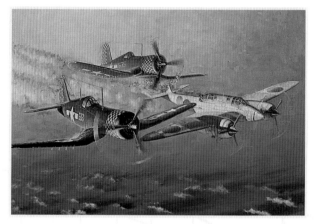

In a personal interview, Durr researched Reusser's memorabilia, and started a research crosscheck with his military records, log books, and printed material.

On May 10, 1945, then-Capt. Ken Reusser of Marine Fighter Squadron VMF- 312 was on his second World War II combat tour. Leading four F4U Corsairs, "Kannibal Ken" took off from Kadena, Okinawa, in a predawn launch. The mission's goal was the destruction of the "Nick."

Reusser had devised a plan that would give the heavy F4U Corsairs an advantage. Removing all weight that could be taken from the fighters to lighten them for a high-altitude climb and waxing the fuselages to reduce drag, the formation of four clawed for altitude before the Nick made its anticipated appearance. Only two of the four, Reusser and his wingman, then-1st Lt. Bob Klingman, were able to keep climbing after the enemy was sighted.

Despite having gained the initiative and being able to pull into a firing position on the Nick's tail, they were horrified to discover that the extreme cold of the unfamiliarly high altitude had caused Reusser's guns to freeze. Pushing to take the only advantage remaining, Reusser tightened up and, with his spinning propeller, chewed the enemy's vertical stabilizer.

When Klingman signaled that he could pull into a firing position, Reusser moved aside. Klingman's guns proved to be frozen, too; but fortunately, so were the guns of the enemy. Klingman's propeller finished the job that Reusser had started. The Nick cartwheeled down and away. The destruction of this particular reconnaissance craft drastically reduced subsequent kamikaze attacks and a Navy Cross was awarded to Reusser for his actions as a squadron division leader on May 10, 1945. ©*Alex Durr*

ONE FINAL THOUGHT

The design configuration of the aircraft you are drawing may be well known to some who view your artwork. Strive for reasonable accuracy in portrayals of historic moments and in any portraits of aircraft; yet, don't neglect the tension, the apprehension, and the mood of suspense that accompanies harrowing flights nor the ecstasy that can be felt in a magical and pleasurable flight. You are learning to draw aircraft and are hopefully on the way to truthfulness and competency in artistic representation. Failure to convey feeling is a failure to interest and involve your viewer.

F6F Desert Hellcat
©Konrad Hack, ASAA

Discovered at Davis-Monthan Air Force Base at the Military Aircraft Storage and Disposition Center in Arizona, this forlorn craft had been salvaged. Hack explained: "The aircraft had crashed into the ocean during World War II. In addition to all the paint having been eaten off, the engine and cowling were bent. I felt the plane had character, standing there all propped up, yet abandoned, forgotten in the desert. I was left with patterns and textures that inspired me. She spoke to me more of her majesty than the combat role that she played."

Drawing, a Foundation
Konrad F. Hack, ASAA

Drawing is of primary importance to a representational artist. ASAA Artist Fellow Konrad Hack said: "Drawing is the first teacher of observation. It is the basic foundation with which to convey structure and form. Drawing is the basis for all painting. One cannot save a bad drawing with paint."

Hack, who teaches drawing and practices what he preaches, knows that there are no shortcuts to learning to draw. Some artists emphasize that you must observe in order to draw, while Hack suggests that you draw in order to learn to observe.

"My secondary concern," says Hack, "is good composition—getting a drawing completed that will hold together and have impact as a shape or movement. The drawing and composition are the skeleton of every work of art."

Hack carries a sketchbook and uses it regularly. His sketchbook provides stimulus to observation and also helps him to recall important details when he starts to improve on a sketched composition. He said: "The camera is an important tool for gathering information to support my ideas and to supplement my sketchbook. But, it is only that—a tool. Firsthand observation and sketching are essential bases to good drawing. To develop a composition, I combine several photos with sketches. I make numerous thumbnail sketches on Vellum, working out the best balance of shape and form, working positive and negative space. Vellum gives me versatility in overlaying my sketches.

"Finally, it depends upon the use of color," explained Hack, "to create a mood. Good use of color can heighten and develop an interesting painting."

Forget-Me-Not
©Konrad Hack, ASAA

Hack's drawing is of the SPAD XIII discovered at the Garber Facility of the Smithsonian's National Air and Space Museum. This particular SPAD, from the 20th Pursuit Squadron, was one of the last airplanes to see combat in the great war, still proudly bearing the original canvas patches over bullet holes sustained during her short but distinguished career. "I took photographs," said Hack, "as I crawled around the wings, careful not to touch her or to disturb this fragile piece of aviation history. I mentally formulated the multitude of possible artworks that could result from this wondrous encounter. This beauty spoke to me of the past and reminded me of how she survived both combat and the ravages of time.

45

"**A**n image can be indicated without drawing an outline. Draw the background, contrast light against dark, and the aircraft shape emerges." *Andy Whyte, ASAA*

SKETCHING AND LINE DRAWING

Drawing Is a Skill, to Be Learned

Students in beginning art classes often are launched by their teachers directly into creating full-color paintings. This approach might be more fun, but it can be lead to frustration or, worse, to giving up art completely because so many required skills have to be mastered at once. If you are serious about learning the challenging skill of art, forget color until you have mastered the skill of drawing.

Basic to most art, drawing forms the cornerstone upon which painting can rest. Drawing can be a prelude to a more finished work (and, as a rule, the most successful paintings are begun as good drawings) or drawing can be an end in itself. Using deft lines, a full range of values, good shapes, positive and negative areas, and good perspective, a drawing can be equated with a fine painting.

Drawing is a skill, to be learned. Anyone with manual dexterity and the desire can learn to draw. It is important to recognize that there are no shortcuts.

Andy Whyte sketched live models quickly to capture a human figure at a moment in time; sketches can help you emphasize body positions, actions, or articles of clothing for later improved drawings or paintings. ©*Andy Whyte, ASAA*

 More finished and more detailed sketches of a person at a moment in time. Note that there are very few straight lines to the human figure. ©Andy Whyte, ASAA

SKETCHING

Start with a sketchpad and some pencils. Train your skills of observation. Learn to look and to really *see*. Choose a variety of subjects—human figures, aircraft, airport buildings, gas trucks, and so forth—and fill your sketchpads with rapidly drawn studies, sketches of shapes that are interesting to you. Sketching can be an excellent way to develop your ability to catch the essence of a scene or an object. The intent is not to achieve an elaborate or finished drawing, but to quickly capture essential features that can serve the artist as guidelines and inspiration. Sketching helps to train the hand and the eye. Sketches can be of any size and, done outdoors and on scene, can capture elusive shapes that might not easily be reconstructed in the studio or after the moment has passed. Thumbnail sketches as preliminary drawings are useful forms of preparation for compositions.

A sketch is a concise and brief drawing that summarizes an idea.

The shading added in these sketches adds depth, shadow, value, and dimension to the figures shown. The sketch of the landing gear shows a range of values in the pencil strokes and demonstrates an ellipse, a challenge to aviation artists who consistently are faced with drawing circular forms. ©Andy Whyte, ASAA

LINE DRAWING

In its simplest form, line drawing is that expressed by line alone. With little attempt to distinguish between light and dark, line drawings express understatement. In addition to perspective and foreshortening, line drawing uses differing weights of particular lines to create or to emphasize depth.

Lines define shape. Straight or curved, delicate or bold, lines can be visible or can be created in the eye of the viewer by the use of shading. Lines drawn horizontally, vertically, or on the diagonal suggest mood, emotion, or movement. With crosshatching, shading, and rubbing, lines can create shadows, depth, and an entire range of values.

Form, shadow, and highlights can be indicated by tints and shading. Darker masses are created by areas of many lines and by drawing lines of heavier width. Emotional effects can result by using short, jagged lines versus the use of broad, sweeping curves.

Because form is the foundation of visual arts, drawing is essential to an artist. Choosing what to depict and what to omit is the artist's challenge.

DRAWING TECHNIQUE

Training the eye to *see* is essential to drawing successfully. Discipline yourself to repeatedly sketch new drawings, fresh angles of familiar subjects, and, for practice, studies of problem areas in drawings. Although your primary reference material for aircraft will be photographs, remember that there is no substitute for sketching from life. Although on-the-spot sketching can be frustrating at times as people or aircraft might not remain stationary, quick drawings can be an excellent practice in developing your ability to catch the essence of a scene.

↓ This sketch, done at Naval Air Station Miramar, shows F-14 Tomcats against the background mountains. The use of midrange values for the mountains establishes the distance from the aircraft. ©*Andy Whyte, ASAA*

Start with the Shape, the Silhouette
Paul Rendel, ASAA

A pilot and an aircraft builder, artist Paul Rendel exemplifies the spirit of the Experimental Aircraft Association (EAA) with his combination of creative talent and technical expertise. He has built his own Thorp-T-18 from plans and he has earned the title of EAA Master Artist at the annual AirVenture Convention and Fly-In.

His skills as a builder provided him with a platform from which to experience the special conditions of flight and the visions of the sky and earth that only flying can provide. As his aviation art attests, he has learned a great deal from his experiences.

An industrial illustrator, trained at the Detroit Institute of Arts and with many years of freelance experience, Paul said that he found himself becoming "artistically boxed into a nook and cranny, relying on old formulae, old techniques." He credits his interactions with other ASAA artists with the kinds of communication that enabled him "to start growing and thinking again." An Artist Fellow member of ASAA and, having served as treasurer, vice president, and president, he has been an active contributor to the organization's success.

Evening Flight shows the beauty of the Allegheny farmland in lengthening shadow, a "lush environment for a Super Cub and a moment in time that a pilot will never forget." ©*Paul Rendel, ASAA*

One artistic technique that Rendel uses is the silhouette. He said: "Many artists want to start drawing details, hoping the completed work will end up as a masterpiece. The correct way is just the opposite. Start with the overall shape or silhouette of the subject. If your drawing is correct, it will be easier to place the details." He also recommends leaving the placement of some of the details to the viewer, taking an artistic approach rather than that of a camera. He said: "Remember, the choices you make will distinguish you as an artist from others. The camera deals with what is, the creative artist deals with what it could be."

Rendel sees his aviation art as that of the storyteller. He believes that "a good painting starts with a vision of a moment in time, supported by the truth, it seeks an emotional response." His aviation art has invariably met that goal.

Meanest in the Valley

Paul Burrows wrote: "This painting combines recollections I have of South Vietnam in 1968–1969. As a Forward Air Controller, I controlled F4s on air strikes many times. On one occasion, during a visual reconnaissance mission, I saw a tiger from about 1,000 feet of altitude. The tiger charged across a clearing about 80 meters wide and disappeared into the trees in about five seconds! Big, fast, and orange! I don't know what he was after, but I'm sure nothing was after him!" ©*Paul Burrows*

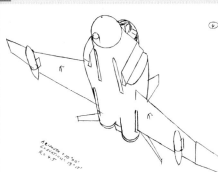

After having chosen the aircraft that will be the focus of a drawing, try to view the craft on the ground and in the air. Analyze the important structural forms of the craft and, with rapid strokes, sketch its essential shapes. View the craft from several vantage points and become so familiar with it that its structure becomes committed to memory. Having sketched the basic outline shapes, then add important details, leaving minor details until last.

American Society of Aviation Artists (ASAA) founder Keith Ferris believes that a person with enough information can draw anything. He also insists that, to draw well, one has to look very carefully and accurately assess what is seen. He said, "An artist must train his or her memory and critical eye. Start with analysis. With an airplane, for example, estimate the length: the nose may stick out for a quarter of the length, the chord of the wing, another quarter. Figure it out. Investigate the aircraft very carefully while challenging yourself with questions. How was it built? What about the control surfaces, the proportions, the various parts? Start thinking three-dimensionally. Where is the light, the cast shadow? Everything that you see can be pictured in terms of light and shadow, lines and spaces, verticals and horizontals. You train yourself to analyze what you see and you are actually seeing more than anybody else."

VALUES

Varied gradations of light and dark are known as values. These are not limited to color paintings, but can be achieved with gradations in the black and the white tones of the drawing.

Value, according to *Compton's Encyclopedia*, "is the amount of light reflected by a surface." Although some value scales differ in their assigned numbers, our study of values begins with a scale from black—assigned a value of 1—to white—assigned a value of 10. The graying process from black to white moves numerically through that scale.

Values are at the core of all artworks. Values gradually change, from black (a low value) and the darkest dark through gray to white (a high

1
2
3
4
5
6
7
8
9
10

Value scale

◀ Values are essential to all works of art. Ranging from black, at the low numbered end of the scale (1), to white, at the high end (10), values encompass the darkest darks to the lightest lights. The value scale applies to colors as well as to black, white, and the intermediate shades of gray. ©*Andy Whyte, ASAA*

7
6
5
4
3
4
2

◀ Using a full range of values will enable an artist to transform a flat circle into a solid sphere. ©*Andy Whyte, ASAA*

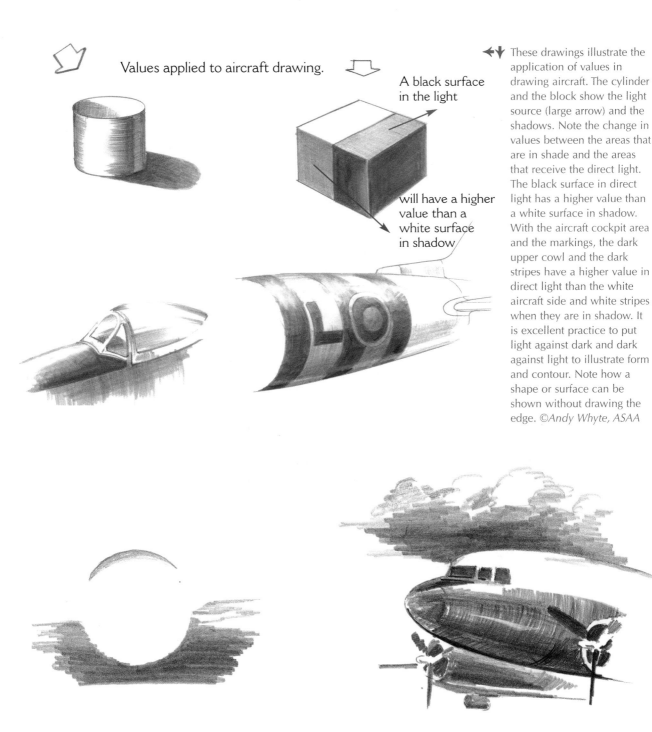

Values applied to aircraft drawing.

A black surface in the light

will have a higher value than a white surface in shadow

These drawings illustrate the application of values in drawing aircraft. The cylinder and the block show the light source (large arrow) and the shadows. Note the change in values between the areas that are in shade and the areas that receive the direct light. The black surface in direct light has a higher value than a white surface in shadow. With the aircraft cockpit area and the markings, the dark upper cowl and the dark stripes have a higher value in direct light than the white aircraft side and white stripes when they are in shadow. It is excellent practice to put light against dark and dark against light to illustrate form and contour. Note how a shape or surface can be shown without drawing the edge. ©Andy Whyte, ASAA

value) and the lightest light. This value scale applies to all color pigments as well; a pale red or a pale blue will have a value as surely as a pale gray. Form is expressed by values. Key to creating form are *contour* and *shadow*.

When a drawing or a painting is viewed, higher values (lighter lights) come forward while lower values (darker darks) recede. Perspective and how the viewer's eyes move throughout the work are controlled by the adjustment of values.

More examples of how values define the forms and contours of an aircraft and its characteristic components. The use of the lowest values or darkest darks and highest values or lightest lights will help to move the viewer's eye to dominant features. ©Andy Whyte, ASAA

The adjustment of values in this drawing of an F4U Corsair helps to attract the viewer's eye to a dominant characteristic, one that is easily identifiable, the gull-shaped wing. ©Andy Whyte, ASAA

↑ These highly detailed drawings of an A-4 Skyhawk illustrate the full range of values and their use in defining form, curvature, and depth. Note again how the eye is drawn to the darkest darks and the lightest lights. ©Andy Whyte, ASAA

Choose a simple subject for your first drawings. Learn that the direction of the pencil strokes can contribute to depth, especially when considering the number of curved lines that are found in an aircraft. Ensure that your lines follow the curves that you are establishing as form. Initially, start with an outline, knowing that you can create that outline with shading as you gain experience.

Establish the tonal values for your drawing, noting the location of the darkest darks and the lightest lights. Build up tone with the point of the pencil as well as the flattened edge. Practice pencil strokes on a separate piece of paper until you have some experience with the weight of lines and ability to draw curves with confidence. An artwork should contain a full range of values, but a single form should be limited to as few values as possible. Use the darkest darks and the lightest lights for the dominant features of the artwork and, especially in aviation art for creating depth and atmosphere. Know that strong foreground darks contrasted with lighter distant darks will enhance desired spatial relationships. To make a shape recede in space, its value should be similar to the value of other items placed at the same distance. Keep the areas of light and shadow simple.

Hang onto your motivation and desire to draw. Keep your sketchpad handy and draw at every opportunity. As you train your eye to see, you will also be training your eye-to-hand coordination and developing your own style. Draw, draw, and *draw!*

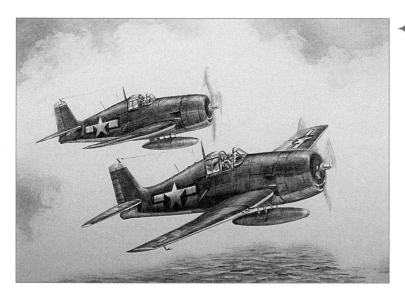

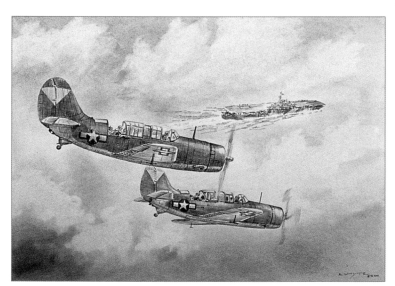

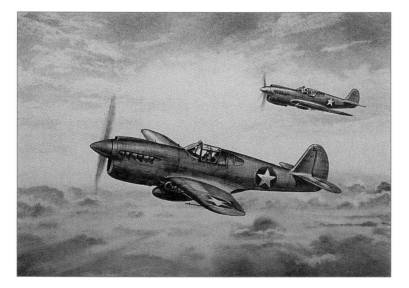

◀▼ (left) (F6Fs), (left middle) (SB2Cs), (left bottom) (P-40s), (below) (F9F), and (below) (SBDs)— These highly detailed drawings of some well-known Warbirds are excellent examples of how deft lines, a full range of values, good shapes, positive and negative areas, and good perspective create black-and-white images that are the equals of fine paintings. ©Andy Whyte, ASAA

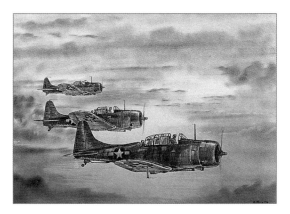

REFERENCE AND RESEARCH MATERIALS

Material Is Readily Available Crosscheck the Facts

s an artist, you aren't 'self-made.' Your work is based on the accumulation of the work of other artists throughout the centuries and what you have learned from what they have done." Andy Whyte, ASAA

USING THE SENSES

To draw, study the art that has been produced over the centuries. An unending supply of art books and museum collections can give you inspiration and education. To draw aircraft, visit the growing numbers of aviation-focused museums and some of the hundreds of air shows and exhibitions at which an artist can be treated to a wide variety of aircraft for observation, sketching, and photographing. Visit local airports to watch aircraft or, better yet, to fly. Take an introductory flight or take flight lessons, see flying from the ground and from the air. Investigate the Experimental Aircraft Association and become involved with a local chapter, learning about aviation from the builders of plans- and kit-built aircraft. If military aircraft operate from nearby, get a visitor's pass to find a location on the flight line from which to observe, to photograph, and to sketch.

The more you know and learn about aviation, the more authenticity you will bring to your aviation drawings. Visit an airfield early in the morning to see highlights reflecting the natural sunlight and the shadows cast. Visit the same airfield late in the day to see the changes in the evening light. Walk around parked aircraft to select the best angle from which to depict the craft and the unique shapes that make it interesting and identifiable. Notice the personnel, trucks, cars, mechanic's carts, gasoline cans, bicycles, flags, windsocks, control towers, and hangars that can add interest to your drawings. Try to see aircraft on display *and* in dynamic action.

For additional information, visit a bookstore and the local library for images and descriptions that will enhance your knowledge. Use the services of research librarians in major aviation museums; most generally respond to a written request, some respond to an electronically mailed request or a telephone call, and some provide research assistance at no cost. The Internet has a wealth of information available with a myriad of aviation-related websites. Military archives such as those at Maxwell Air Force Base, at NASA, or at the National Archives in Washington, D.C., are responsive to legitimate research requests.

For the human factor that adds interest to your drawings, look into groups and clubs that might be located near your home and studio. There are re-enactors who put on military displays, complete with the uniforms, weapons, aircraft, and utensils. There are retired military enlistees and officers who will share stories with you—their

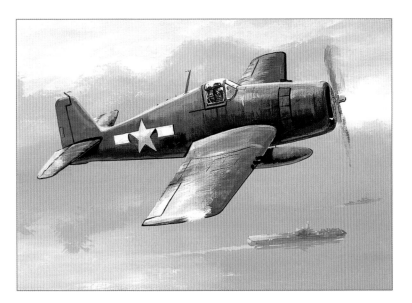

◀ Beware of copying photographs. Unless the drawing and the photograph are depicted from the same viewing point, distortion will result. Note the difference in the sizes of the wings in this F6F Hellcat, a distortion that could have been avoided. ©*Andy Whyte, ASAA*

experiences, their scrapbooks, and their photographs. People who populate the local airport are generally eager to talk about aviation—a dynamic career field and exciting activity.

USING CAMERAS AND PHOTOGRAPHS

Be wary! Although the use of the camera and photographs has become second nature to the artist, there are some advantages and some pitfalls to this medium. Use photographs as reference material only. Know, too, that the eye that spends too much time behind the camera viewfinder is *not* being properly trained to *see*.

Some Dos and Don'ts:

DO try to be the one to take the photographs that you use. That will enhance their use as reference and you will have the advantage of choosing the lighting, distance, and lens.

DO recognize that your photo is most accurate when the eye level in the drawing corresponds to the position of the camera in the photo.

DO know that, in using a photograph for reference, you should work out the perspective of the photographic image and its translation to the picture plane.

DO use a monopod for photographing airborne propeller-driven aircraft. This steadies your hand while using a telephoto lens and shooting at the slower shutter speeds that prevent "stopping" the propeller action—1/250th or 1/125th of a second.

DO know that perspective is related to distance from the subject. Take photos in which the image in the viewfinder corresponds with the image you wish to depict in your drawing.

DON'T copy photographs. This is especially true when you are not the person who took the photo! It is plagiarism to copy a photographer's shot.

DON'T trace photographs. Distortions can creep into your drawings. It is better to learn to train the eye and the hand.

Quote

"The more you know and learn about aviation, the more authenticity you will bring to your aviation drawings."

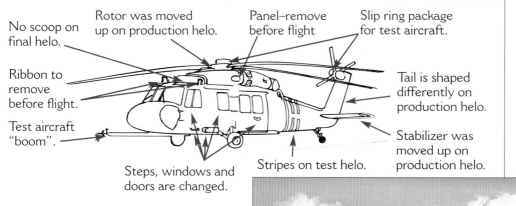

No scoop on final helo.

Rotor was moved up on production helo.

Panel–remove before flight

Slip ring package for test aircraft.

Ribbon to remove before flight.

Test aircraft "boom".

Tail is shaped differently on production helo.

Stabilizer was moved up on production helo.

Steps, windows and doors are changed.

Stripes on test helo.

↟ This outline drawing of the UH-60 initial prototype is labeled to show the major changes that were needed/made to the helicopter as it progressed from the prototype stage to the operational, or production, model. ©Andy Whyte, ASAA

➜ Here's an example of using a photograph as reference for a drawing without checking the validity of the research. This UH-60 Blackhawk is the initial prototype, a one-of-a-kind aircraft that is not a production model. ©Andy Whyte, ASAA

USING MODEL AIRCRAFT

Building model aircraft can be a good step toward understanding the form and parts of any aircraft and enhancing the awareness of how engineering challenges have been met. The act of creating a model from a kit can be satisfying and educational.

Using the model should be secondary to analyzing the real craft. Models can help to reinforce some of the important structural components that are not shown in photographic reference material. Taking a model aircraft outside during the particular time of day and particular weather conditions that are desired for the drawing can help to show cast shadows and how shadows and reflected light highlight the craft. The model can be turned to various angles and attitudes to determine the craft's most interesting view or to show less appealing views and flight attitudes that might obscure some aircraft parts. Model aircraft can be decorative and helpful tools. Refer to them and build them for a greater appreciation of the real aircraft, but know their limitations.

Some Dos and Don'ts:

DO consider building model aircraft to enhance your knowledge and increase your enjoyment of aviation.

DO use model aircraft to help you with spatial relationships.

DO learn from radio-controlled model aircraft and from builders of those flying models.

DO use model aircraft to experiment with light and shadow, curved surfaces, and for inspiration and ideas.

DON'T assume that model aircraft are completely accurate.

DON'T forget the rigidity of airfoils and how they differ from the more flexible airfoils on actual aircraft.

DON'T limit your research for a drawing to a model aircraft alone.

ADDING HUMAN MODELS

In addition to numerous groups who collect uniforms, equipment, weaponry, and the accoutrements of the U.S. Civil War and the Revolutionary War, there are re-enactors who stage mock battles and historic scenes from World War I and World War II. Often, these models are knowledgeable of their period and can help in adding authenticity to a proposed drawing. World War I re-enactors gather biennially at the U.S. Air Force Museum in Dayton, Ohio, and, in addition to being well equipped with uniforms and military paraphernalia, they boast more than 20 flying replica aircraft of the World War I era. In Rhinebeck, New York, the late Cole Palen amassed a wealth of flying aircraft that date to the World War I era, several of which are original, and many of the performers dress in vintage outfits to entertain and educate visitors.

Use of models and re-enactors gives the artist a chance to draw from life. To view the subtleties of the human figure in a variety of poses offers an artist a vast improvement over the use of photographs. If you *must* use photographs, be certain that you first have learned to draw the human figure and are using the photos for reference.

PLAYING SLEUTH, UNCOVERING THE STORY

Libraries, museums, archives, military bases, universities, squadron historians, professional researchers, and aviation organizations are out there and willing to help you with research. When you meet someone who has a great aviation story that inspires an image in your imagination, there are numerous places you can go to back that story up and crosscheck the facts. Do your homework and get the facts straight.

Arm yourself with more informa-

↑ *The Crewman* is a fine example of a drawing from life of the human figure. It began as a study for another painting and now stands alone as a fine artwork. ©*Gil Cohen, ASAA*

↓ Doing your research homework carefully and completely is vital. Although it may look familiar, this aircraft does not exist. Unless your purpose is to depict an imaginary aircraft, be sure that you represent your subject accurately. Aviation art enthusiasts tend to be knowledgeable, precise, and technical. ©*Andy Whyte, ASAA*

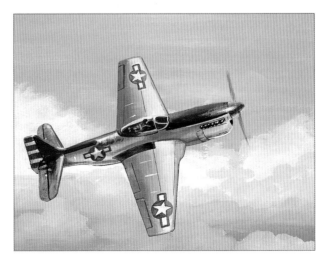

Doing a Little Research

Gerald Asher, ASAA

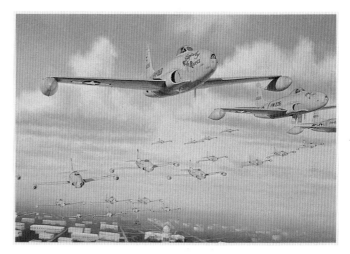

Asked by the Air Force Association in early 1997 to create a painting that would depict "Early Jet Aviation" for its upcoming USAF 50th Anniversary calendar, Gerald Asher opted for a subject that actually pre-dated the creation of the Air Force as a separate air arm—the 412th Fighter Group (FG), March Field, California. During May 1946, under the code name *Project Comet*, 29 Lockheed P-80A Shooting Star jet fighters under the command of Col. Bruce K. Holloway participated in a 12-day, nine-city "barnstorming tour" of the United States. The highlight of the 412th FG's mission was a three-day appearance at Washington, D.C., where the unit performed before crowds estimated at 100,000 people.

With a few photos already on file of the unit's aircraft for that period (some taken at Washington National Airport), Asher wanted to get a better conception of the entire mission. As with other research projects he had undertaken, he sunk his teeth into this one and shook it like the proverbial junkyard dog. He examined the mission from every conceivable aspect: official military documents (USAF Historical Research Agency at Maxwell AFB, Alabama) gave the names of many of the mission's pilots. A number were tracked down through the American Fighter Aces Association (nearly all of the 412th pilots were combat veterans) and those contacted helped locate other surviving unit members. Respectfully, Asher made contact with the widows of deceased pilots, many of whom were happy to loan their photo collections.

Newspaper photos and articles at the stopover points for *Project Comet*, which he accessed through correspondence with local libraries and newspaper morgues, included more valuable information. Even blind phone calls to locate surviving local residents, in some cases, were fruitful beyond his expectations.

At the end of it all, Asher had more than enough information to accomplish his painting and was confident that he had a clear understanding of his subject. In his opinion, that's the most important aspect of a painting project—it's what keeps the work from being "just another airplane picture."

tion than you need—time of day, weather conditions, specific type of aircraft, crew members aboard, clothing worn, and pertinent facts that led to the outcome of the scene. Check and crosscheck the facts. Conduct interviews, search for specifics like the insignia on the aircraft and the color scheme of any tail markings. Know the story, know the moment when the story unfolded, and decide on the purpose for the drawing.

Then, simplify. Draw hasty sketches that underscore the important facts and keep the drawing uncluttered and specific. Become involved with the emotions of the moment and seek to involve and intrigue your viewer. Draw the image that you'd like to see; tell the story that you want told.

The Human Factor

Gil Cohen, ASAA

Gil Cohen said: "Figures are what the art of most artists is all about. If you want to learn to draw the figure, you are going to have to draw the figure from life. Copying a photograph does not make it easier; it makes it more difficult. A photo is a flat image. It cannot possibly show the range of tones and colors that the human eye can see. More importantly, we see in three dimensions and the camera does *not* do that. Learn that the photo is *not* going to do it for you *unless you already know how to draw!*"

Preliminary pencil sketch for the composition. ©*Gil Cohen, ASAA*

Cohen links aviation developments with humans. He said, "An aircraft wouldn't *fly* if it weren't for the persons who designed it, who built it, who maintained it, who took to the skies in it!"

In studying history, Cohen believes that it's as if "we're reading the last page first. We *know* the outcome. Combatants who were fighting wars had no idea as to the outcome of their battles. I approach history as it was at the *moment*. I want to show heartfelt emotions and have my viewers feel those emotional responses as well. I don't like to glamorize anything having to do with war. Men would have exhibited apprehension and uncertainty, some fear and some giddy elation. The machines would have been grimy, faded, and oil-streaked."

Cohen begins a painting with small pencil sketches. Emulating Konstantin Stanislavsky, the film director who created "the method" and held that an actor's main responsibility was to be believed, Cohen hires re-enactors to wear World War II uniforms and model for him. Placing them in and around aircraft and preparing to take a myriad of photographs, he directs them with thoughts and actions that create responses and emotions.

"From among the poses that you achieve," said Cohen, "select those that contribute to the painting. Compositionally, it should not be monotonous. Every figure must contribute to the mood that is to be depicted."

At the U.S. Air Force Museum, Ohio, he posed and directed models in the cramped front section of a B-17. To create the realities of a bomb run for the navigator and the bombardier, he emphasized to the models his need for them to express a gamut of emotions—a fatalistic determination, exhaustion, an anticipation laced with fear, and/or a proud sense of duty. He watched their bodies, the lift to the chin, or the dropping of the eyes. He gave them suggestions as to what they might be feeling as he photographed each pose and watched for specific emotions in gestures, in body stance, and in his models' eyes. Cohen's research resulted in the fine art painting *Mission Regensburg*.

Cohen wanted to portray the navigator and bombardier and to draw his viewer into the scene with the two crew members. He sketched bombardiers and navigators manning their positions and also machine guns—the least qualified gunners manning machines in the most vulnerable place in that aircraft.

He researched the nose section of the B-17G, photographed the forward

Completed acrylic underpainting.
©*Gil Cohen, ASAA*

Oil overpainting detail.
©*Gil Cohen, ASAA*

Mission Regensburg, **completed painting.** ©*Gil Cohen, ASAA*

smaller window, the bombardier's chair, Norden bombsight, and machine guns. He obtained factory shots of the B-17 with the mechanical apparatus that he wanted and had help with details about the navigator by interviewing Harry Crosby, a World War II B-17 navigator who wrote *Wing and a Prayer*, and, incidentally, is left-handed, as Cohen showed in his painting. He located a good navigator's computer, penlight, 50-caliber machine gun bullets, ammo, chute, goggles, navigational map, and so forth.

When his composition began to jell, he made larger, more detailed drawings on tracing paper. His drawings are intended as preliminaries to a finished painting, but each is a unique work of art itself. After he started drawing on canvas, he said, "I wanted the viewer to be almost dazzled by the light coming through the windows and left those areas that would be brightest in the picture. I was doing a symphony and couldn't settle for a string quartet."

GETTING THE RIGHT PERSPECTIVE

Portraying Aircraft in Three Dimensions

"Perspective can be a way of trying to visualize an aircraft. It is easier to visualize a box or a cube, so take the basic aircraft and divide it into a set of boxes. This can be a first step toward proper perspective." *Andy Whyte, ASAA*

By developing linear perspective in the first half of the fifteenth century, Italy's Filippo Brunelleschi spawned the art of mathematical perspective. That physical space can be reduced to mathematical principles and analysis, to terms of proportion and perspective, continues to challenge artists to this day. Perspective drawing aims to represent the actual three-dimensional aspect of an object and is a matter of scientific determination. In a perspective drawing, an object is shown as it looks to the eye at the given point of view; but a mathematical process determines the exact angles, dimensions, distortion, and foreshortening of each part. To draw aircraft with accurate form, correctly depicting distance, depth, and the proper appearance of objects, practice drawing with proper perspective. A working knowledge of two-point perspective is essential to accuracy.

Aviation artists use a variety of methods to handle proper perspective. The methods range from "eyeballing" to draw shapes that "look right," to using two-point perspective, and to the highly detailed and mathematical system of descriptive geometry.

Proper perspective creates an accurate basis in form. Detail follows form. Perspective is the tool by which the artist properly portrays an aircraft that has height and width and looks, on the flat surface, the way it appears to the naked eye. Proper perspective helps to ensure that a wing or a rotor is not too long or too short.

In perspective drawing, the picture is drawn on a flat surface—the "picture plane." The eye of the viewer is the "station point," and the horizon line that divides the scene is the "eye level." Remember these basics: the *picture plane*, the surface on which you draw your aircraft; the *station point*, the point from which you or your viewer sees your aircraft; the *horizon*, the eye-level line that divides the scene and, in a drawing of an aircraft, can be higher than the craft if the craft is taxiing on the ground or can be below the craft if the craft is airborne; and the *vanishing point or points* that occur on the horizon or eye level and at which all parallel lines of perspective appear to converge.

SINGLE-POINT PERSPECTIVE

In single-point perspective, one side of the object is parallel to the picture plane, and two dimensions, height and width, are shown. One-point perspective is good practice to develop your eye and your technique.

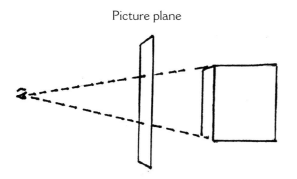

Picture plane

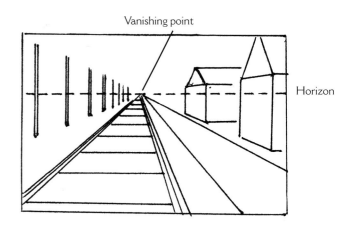

Vanishing point

Horizon

↑ A drawing in one-point perspective shows one side of the object parallel to the picture plane and two dimensions of the object—height and width. ©Andy Whyte, ASAA

↑ The vanishing point is on the horizon (eye level), as shown by the dashed line, and all parallel lines of perspective converge at that point. ©Andy Whyte, ASAA

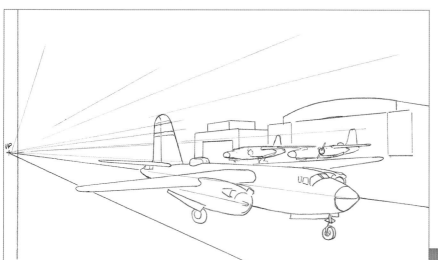

◄↓ Andy Whyte's B-26 Martin Marauder is shown taxiing. He has drawn lines of perspective that converge on the horizon. ©Andy Whyte, ASAA

TWO-POINT PERSPECTIVE

Two-point perspective adds a second and different point on the horizon at which parallel lines converge. It gives a view of two sides and three dimensions of the object, adding depth to the height and the width.

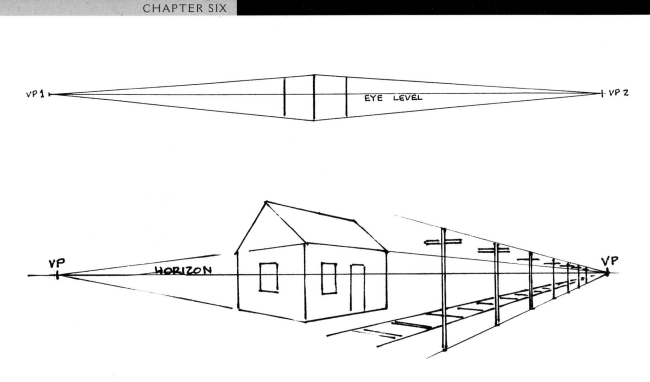

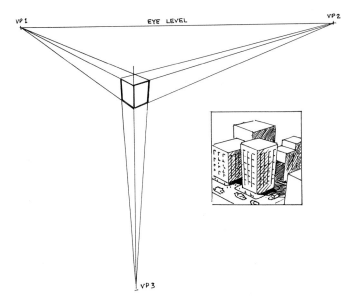

In two-point perspective, we see two sides and three dimensions of the object—height, width, and depth. There are two vanishing points on the horizon. ©Andy Whyte, ASAA

THREE-POINT PERSPECTIVE

Three-point perspective is necessary when the picture plane is tilted, that is, is *not* parallel to any of the three dimensions of the object. Three-point perspective allows a viewer to look *down* upon the object—the third vanishing point converging *below* the picture plane—or to look *upward* toward the subject—the vanishing point converging *above* the picture plane.

Linear perspective depends upon the lines of the drawing to create the illusion of three dimensions and to give objects the proper size and shape. Practice drawing squares, then giving dimensions to the squares to form cubes or boxes.

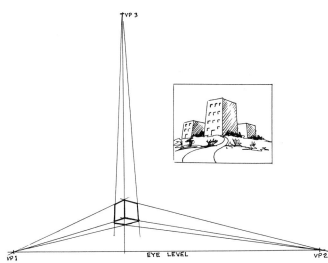

In three-point perspective, the horizon or eye level is either above (6:6) or below (6:7) the object being drawn. Three vanishing points are established. In three-point perspective, the picture plane is tilted. ©Andy Whyte, ASAA

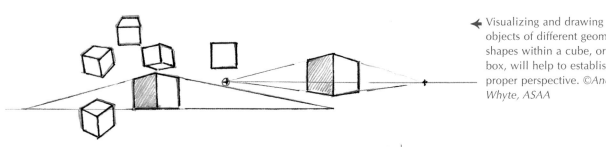

Visualizing and drawing objects of different geometric shapes within a cube, or box, will help to establish proper perspective. ©Andy Whyte, ASAA

As a method for visualizing an airplane, divide the basic airplane into boxes. The set of boxes gives you the proper perspective, drawing the centerline of the airplane like a flat section divided with cross-sectional cuts. Put sections of the airplane into different cubes. The first cube will hold the spinner and the propeller, the second will hold the nose and part of the cockpit, the third will contain the cockpit and the turtle deck, and so on. Draw the portion of each circular shape that is not visible from the selected view. That is important to arrive at a three-dimensional figure.

Basic sizes, shapes, and surface forms are important. Prove the drawing by establishing the vanishing points and be certain that the two horizontal vanishing points are relative to a single horizon, the eye level. Measurement and proportion are important, as is training the eye to recognize both elements.

In order to depict the height, width, and depth of an object in perspective, it is helpful to construct a grid of multiple cubes and to divide those cubes in half with diagonal lines. ©Andy Whyte, ASAA

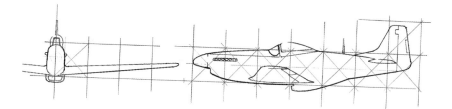

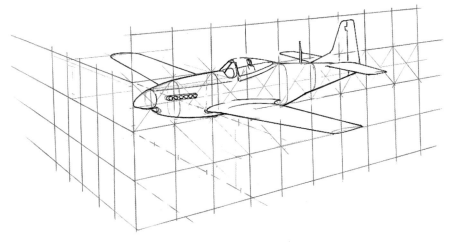

By drawing this P-51 Mustang on the picture plane and within cubes of equal size, the artist can establish the correct size and shape for each of the aircraft's segments. The aircraft can then be turned and put in perspective, maintaining each segment's proper size. Note: As the Mustang is turned to show all three of its dimensions, the segments will decrease in size as they move in the direction of the vanishing points. ©Andy Whyte, ASAA

Descriptive Geometry

Keith Ferris, ASAA Founder

First Trap

At the invitation of U.S. Navy Training Squadron VT-26, based at National Air Station (NAS) Chase Field, Beeville, Texas, Keith Ferris departed on a Rockwell T-2C Buckeye mission enroute to the training carrier CVT-16 *Lexington*, July 14, 1982. Flying with the VT-26 Skipper, the mission was to escort a group of solo T-2C students from NAS Chase to the "Lady Lex" for their *First Trap* (their first arrested landing) and catapult takeoff for carrier qualification. Although Ferris had experienced many, many landings in Air Force jet trainers and fighters, he said, "This was a totally new experience."

The carrier-landing pattern was precise and Ferris timed it at exactly 60 seconds from the beginning of the turn to base opposite the Landing Signal Officer (LSO) and on final to touchdown. He said, "The aircraft ahead was to catch the number three 'wire' only 45 seconds ahead of us. I had the overwhelming feeling of being way too high and way too close to the ship to ever get our 'Buckeye' safely onto that tiny deck."

As their aircraft followed the "ball" down final approach, the other T-2 was still in the way. Yet, the deck cleared and Ferris' T-2 caught the number three "wire" at

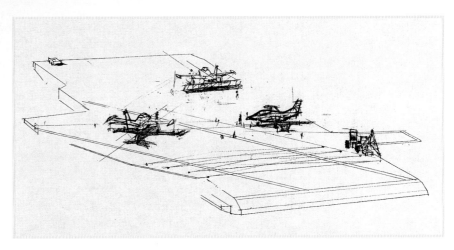

exactly 60 seconds. He said, "That made a lasting impression! I determined that my painting would convey precisely how ship and aircraft would look at approximately halfway through that evolution."

The initial pen and marker drawing, from memory, shows Ferris' basic composition for the painting *First Trap*. The next step was to examine the spatial relationships and timing of the landing pattern. He diagrammed to scale the moving aircraft and ship at their speeds in feet per second. The painting was to depict the 28-second point in the pattern.

Measurements indicated that the ship moved 1,408 feet from the position seen in the painting 32 seconds prior to trap. Deciding upon a painting that measured 28 inches high by 56 inches wide gave Ferris the determination that the preferred viewing position for the painting would be approximately 6 feet. He explained: "Knowing the size of the T-2 planned in the drawing, the visual angle from the eye to extremities was set. This same angle, superimposed on the top view of a three-view drawing, located the top view of the viewer's position relative to the top view of the T-2. This turned out to be 110 feet aft, 34.5 feet right of centerline (CL), and 23.5 feet above the horizontal reference plane. The height of the viewing position was selected to show the solo student and enough of the rear seat to emphasize the solo flight and to show that seat empty."

©Keith Ferris, ASAA

The artist's perspective projection was done by descriptive geometry. Well above the aircraft is a line that is "horizon/line of flight." Because the T-2 is flying at 15 units "angle of attack" (AOA), the horizon drops to eye level through the pilot's head. Ferris showed bank angles of 15, 18, 21, and 25 degrees with the horizons for each bank angle on the drawing. He chose the 18-degree bank angle for the finished painting. He said: "Keeping the viewing position constant, the next move was to plot the *Lexington* from the same viewing position as that selected for the aircraft. The distance from the ship at the 28-second point was determined from the carrier landing evolution diagram."

The *Lexington* is seen from a position 425 feet above sea level, 3,300 feet aft of the LSO, and 500 feet left of the centerline of wake. Ferris said, "Note the telescoped effect, much like that seen with a telephoto lens."

It remained for the artist to combine all of this in small scale and to project onto the gessoed canvas for completion of the finished drawing.

Ferris showed the four "pendants" or wires across the deck. His drawings were traced into position onto the canvas and refined with all the other details of the ship and primary T-2C aircraft. He had to analyze the lighting, establish the background, and begin the actual oil painting. For detailed reference, he projected, above his easel, the many slides that he had taken of the aircraft, ship, water, and wake during his time aboard the vessel with VT-26.

The training of his critical eye has been highly successful to Ferris. In calling on his sense of the geometry of flight, he has pictured a sweeping, descending arc from entry into the traffic pattern to touchdown. He said, "Flying is a beautiful aerial ballet and the geometry is something that can be totally visualized."

Ferris paints with a limited palette—the three primary colors plus white. He learned early in his career to avoid copying any photographs. He creates all of his own drawings by freehand, construction by analysis, or perspective projection by descriptive geometry. He maintains an exhaustive research library that includes flight handbooks, maintenance and tech manuals, his own collection of approximately 50,000 cross-indexed slides, insignia of squadrons that he has flown with in the past 35 years, and innumerable books, magazines, and photographs. When Ferris begins to create a new painting, he selects his subject, creates thumbnails for a composition that pleases him, searches his files for material on the subject aircraft, and pulls together the material in quick oil color studies. In his painstaking way, he determines the average viewing position and sets the visual angle from the viewer to the painting.

The description of his creation of *First Trap* is not unique. Ferris, who has been called the "Precise Painter," uses the same careful research, analysis, planning, and painterly construction in all of his paintings.

➤ To draw a house in perspective, first draw a horizontal line to represent the picture plane (PP). Make certain that the closest corner of the house touches the PP. Select a station point (SP), an arbitrary point from which the house is to be viewed. Draw lines from the SP to the PP that are parallel to the sides of the house and are at 90 degrees to one another. These points of intersection on the PP will be used to define the vanishing points (VPs) by dropping a vertical line from each to the horizon line.

From the corners of the house, draw straight lines that converge at the SP. When each of these lines reaches the PP, drop a vertical line (shown by the dotted lines) down to the horizon line. This is the technique by which a flat image can be put into perspective and viewed as it would look to the naked eye. ©Andy Whyte, ASAA

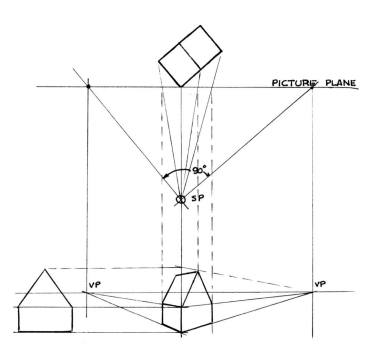

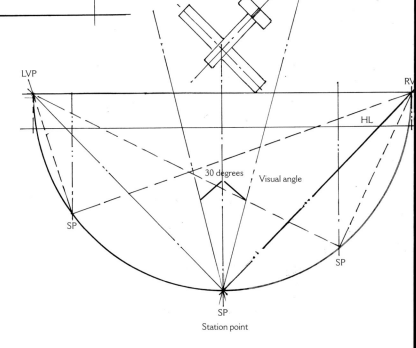

This drawing adds a horizon (eye level) line and additional station points (SPs). To establish vanishing points (VPs), vertical lines are carried from the picture plane (PP) to the horizon line. Note that the VPs are the same when the SPs are equidistant from the center of the aircraft. Central to this diagram is a 30-degree viewing angle that encompasses the entire aircraft. ©Andy Whyte, ASAA

↑ This initial perspective drawing demonstrates the first step in determining the right and left vanishing points (RVPs and LVPs). From the chosen station point (SP), the view selected by the artist, lines from the SP to the picture plane (PP) are drawn parallel to the centerline of the fuselage and the centerline of the wing—a 90-degree angle at the SP. At the intersection of those lines on the PP, vertical lines are then carried to the horizon where the RVP and LVP will be located. ©Andy Whyte, ASAA

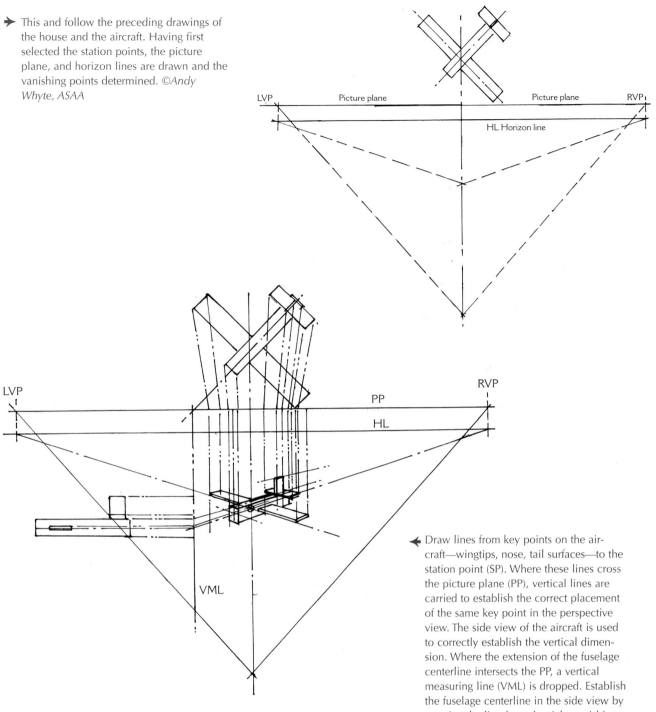

→ This and follow the preceding drawings of the house and the aircraft. Having first selected the station points, the picture plane, and horizon lines are drawn and the vanishing points determined. ©Andy Whyte, ASAA

◄ Draw lines from key points on the aircraft—wingtips, nose, tail surfaces—to the station point (SP). Where these lines cross the picture plane (PP), vertical lines are carried to establish the correct placement of the same key point in the perspective view. The side view of the aircraft is used to correctly establish the vertical dimension. Where the extension of the fuselage centerline intersects the PP, a vertical measuring line (VML) is dropped. Establish the fuselage centerline in the side view by carrying the line from the right vanishing point (VP) through the viewing point at the center of the aircraft to the VML. Other vertical dimensions are then determined. The horizontal dimensions can be determined similarly with respect to the left vanishing point (LVP) and the VP using the leading edge of the wing. The lines from the VPs through the centerlines of the fuselage and the wings position the perspective view correctly. ©Andy Whyte, ASAA

DESCRIPTIVE GEOMETRY

In 1527, Albrecht Dürer introduced the mathematical method of representing three-dimensional forms on a two-dimensional surface—descriptive geometry. In 1795, Gaspard Monge perfected Dürer's remarkable achievement in applying mathematics to art. Descriptive geometry is used in all branches of engineering. Mechanical drawing and architectural elevations are based on the principles of descriptive geometry, a mathematically precise way to establish perspective.

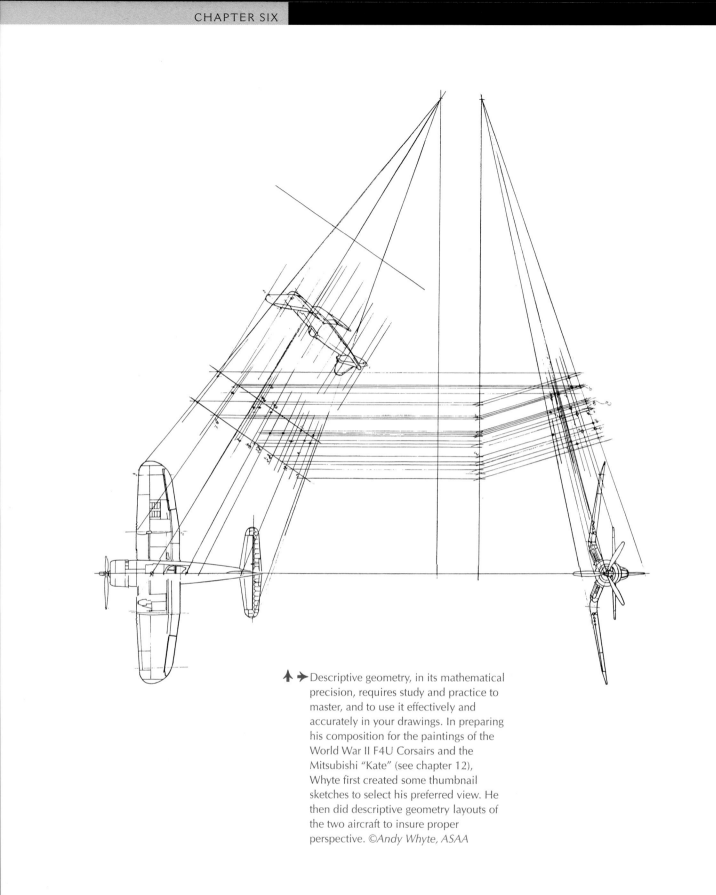

➤ ➤ Descriptive geometry, in its mathematical
precision, requires study and practice to
master, and to use it effectively and
accurately in your drawings. In preparing
his composition for the paintings of the
World War II F4U Corsairs and the
Mitsubishi "Kate" (see chapter 12),
Whyte first created some thumbnail
sketches to select his preferred view. He
then did descriptive geometry layouts of
the two aircraft to insure proper
perspective. ©Andy Whyte, ASAA

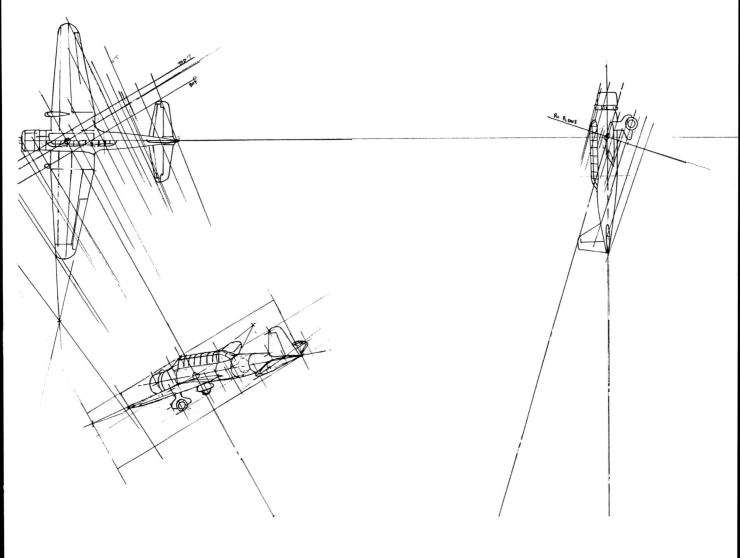

CIRCLE AND ELLIPSE

A circle is a plane figure bounded by a single curved line every point of which is equidistant from the center. An ellipse is a circle at any angle except when viewed at 90 degrees; in other words, an ellipse is a circle drawn to perspective. Start by drawing a cylinder or a cone.

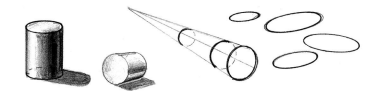

↑ Drawing aircraft well requires the ability to draw circular and elliptical figures, flat and rounded surfaces—for example, wheels and tires, engine cowls, jet intakes and exhausts, propeller arcs, canopies, and insignia and airline markings. Use familiar geometric shapes to aid in placing a circle in perspective. ©Andy Whyte, ASAA

Draw a circle within the confines of a cube or box, which is easier to envision, easier to depict, and easier to put into proper perspective. Cross the center with two diagonal lines. Cross the center again with, first, a vertical line and, secondly, a horizontal line through the intersection of the diagonals. Take lines out to a vanishing point to be sure the horizontal through the center is correct. The angle of the axis gives the shape to the ellipse. Remember, the major axis of an ellipse is never vertical unless the center of the circle is on the horizon or eye level.

The renowned British artist Charles Thompson wrote, "Draw a circle onto a flat card and then cut it out. Draw a straight line across the diameter of the card and through the center of the circle. This line represents the MAJOR AXIS. [Draw a second straight line across the diameter of the card at a right angle to the major axis. This line represents the LATERAL AXIS.] Make a small hole in the center and insert a skewer or long cocktail stick, pushing it through for half of the length of the stick. This stick, which appears as an axle of a wheel, represents the MINOR AXIS. . . . To perceive a perfect circle, look directly down the line of the MINOR AXIS or AXLE. . . . Place a finger at each end of the MAJOR AXIS and begin to tilt the plane of the card, pivoting about these two points. The circle will be immediately perceived as an ellipse. . . . The MINOR AXIS (axle) is always drawn at right angles to the major axis."

In drawing a wheel and a tire, first draw a cube into which the circular form fits. Turn that cube, drawing it at the angle that is in proper perspective for the rest of the aircraft. Use the diagonals to find the center point and then draw the portion of the wheel that cannot be seen. That is, draw an ellipse for the top and for the bottom, later eliminating the line that is "behind" the object and out of the viewer's sight.

The Circle Has No End

Nixon Galloway, ASAA

As a founder, with five other illustrators, of Group West, Inc., Nixon Galloway has been a leading West Coast artist in the field of advertising. His experience has been invaluable, having drawn figures, landscapes, architecture, and more. A past president of both the Los Angeles Society of Illustrators and the American Society of Aviation Artists, he has focused on aviation art whenever the chance comes his way. Galloway is a pilot and the grandson of a leading aviation pioneer in the Los Angeles area.

For proper perspective in drawing aircraft, Galloway said: "I usually use two-point perspective (using two vanishing points placed on the horizon line). I find that three-point perspective is rarely necessary, unless you have buildings or vertical objects below your aircraft. Adding some vertical lines along the centerline of the fuselage is handy for reference points for the vertical lines on the airplane such as an antenna, the vertical stabilizer, or winglets. (Know that some of these may or may not be completely vertical in regard to the fuselage.)

"A use of aerial perspective is essential. That refers to the graying and loss of distinction with distance that is a function of atmosphere; it is one method of conveying depth in aviation and aerospace art, which involves such vast distances."

All aircraft have rounded forms. To draw circles and ellipses, Galloway explained, "I use ellipse guides that you can get in art supply stores. They come in 5-degree increments and varying sizes. A 90-degree ellipse would be a circle. An 80-degree ellipse is slightly oval, and through increments, ellipses become narrower ovals—a 10-degree ellipse is very slim and a 0-degee ellipse would be a straight line. As I arrive at the proper ellipse to use, I often note that on the drawing, for future reference."

First Mission
In researching for this painting, Galloway knew that each aircraft had a prominent letter on its side under the cockpit—a code letter. He contacted an Air Force locater service. He explained, "You write a letter to a particular USAF veteran, put it in a stamped envelope, and enclose all of that in another envelope addressed to the USAF Locater Service, Maxwell AFB, in Alabama. If they can find the combat veteran, they will mail the letter for you."

First Mission took place out of England in 1942. Galloway wrote to each of the crew members listed for this flight and, three months later, received a call from Robert Golay, the dorsal gunner. Galloway said, "He told me the code letter was zed, Z. He also answered questions raised in accounts about whether the propeller was shot off or whether it snapped when the aircraft hit the ground. The gunner said, 'I felt us take a hit and saw a propeller go sailing by, just missing the stabilizer. My first thought was, I hope that wasn't ours.' Reaching actual crew members is a gratifying and pleasurable experience." ©*Nixon Galloway, ASAA*

If specific models necessary to a planned artwork were available, Galloway built model airplanes for the knowledge that he gained about the structures and shapes of each part of the craft. He also mentioned some of the pitfalls of using models. He said: "Be very cautious about models. They have their place, but they also have their limitations. Be certain that a reference model is correct. Also keep in mind that most aircraft change when in flight—wings may flex, the gear may extend lower, and jet exhaust nozzles fluctuate. These are physical changes that cannot possibly be indicated by structurally rigid models."

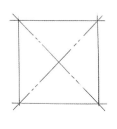
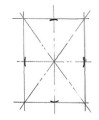
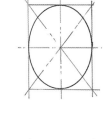

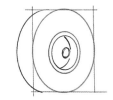

It generally takes several ellipses in drawing aircraft to create curved shapes, i.e., the fuselage. Begin by drawing a rectangular form into which the curved form is fit. The center of the rectangular form is as important as was the center of the square. Divide the surfaces with the cross diagonals to establish the center. Prove the drawing by taking lines of the form toward the vanishing points.

COMPOUND FORMS

Most objects are compound forms—the combination of different cubes, rectangles, and ellipses. For these compound forms, keep the vanishing points farther apart for more pleasing compositions. Always consider the station point, vanishing points, and horizon or eye level. All verticals are truly vertical except when a special effect is desired and a third vanishing point is required. This will be necessary

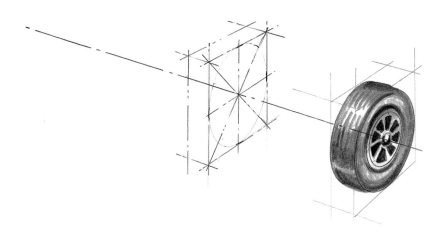

↑ ➤ Note the square seen at eye level with diagonals intersecting to determine the center. Only if seen directly in this square would the figure be a circle. Any other view would result in that circle becoming an ellipse. Draw your circle within a box. Having determined the perspective of the box, you can center the minor axis. Understanding the several axes involved also helps. The major axis is the diameter of a circle and is at a right angle to the lateral axis on the face of the flat circular form. Thinking of the minor axis as the axle of a tire, remember that the minor axis always pierces the center of a circle at a right angle to the major axis. While the length of the major axis remains constant, the lateral axis will vary in length as the circle becomes elliptical in shape. The curved surfaces of the aircraft—fuselage, engine cowling, insignia, and propeller arc—can be put into proper perspective using these techniques.
©Andy Whyte, ASAA

in all flying scenes. Remember, compound forms are not complex, they are just multiples of the square and rectangle with which you have been working.

FORESHORTENING

When adding the human figure to drawings, use perspective to keep all objects relative to every other. Place your figure in the simpler shaped rectangular cube or box. Whether the object is an aircraft wing or a human limb, there is a necessity to foreshorten a form when it is aimed at, or coming toward, or receding from the viewer. A human leg or arm is a free form, a form composed of several pliable curves. Think of the figure as a cube, a cylinder, a sphere, or a cone and keep the perspective in mind. In drawing the figure and most small objects, if the station point is too close to the object, distortion will result. Every form has depth. Every form has perspective.

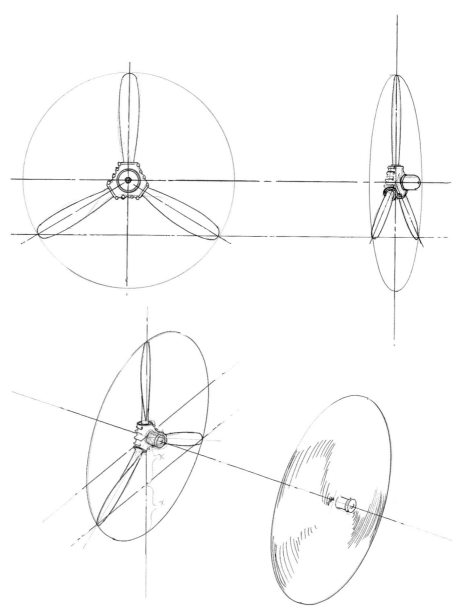

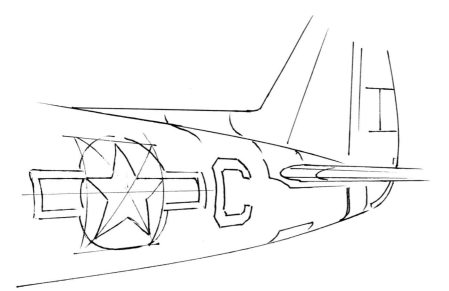

CUTAWAYS
AND SCALE
VIEWS, COCKPITS
AND INTERIORS

➤ A cutaway drawing of a Chance-Vought F4U Corsair with aluminum structural members painted with zinc chromate, a preservative. Note the detail in the engine, the cockpit, the landing gear, and the tail hook for catching the arresting gear on an aircraft carrier. ©Andy Whyte, ASAA

f an artist knows where all the guts are located, where parts are located in relation to others, then the artist has a hint of the knowledge required to portray that subject." *Andy Whyte, ASAA*

CUTAWAY DRAWINGS

Aircraft use moving parts to perform the work that is expected of them. Like other machines, aircraft have parts that are designed to deliver a specific force to cause a resulting specific movement. Some parts are designed to convert one movement to another. For example, a piston moves back and forth with linear movement as a direct reaction to internal combustion. The piston is linked by a connecting rod to cause rotation of the crankshaft, a circular movement that directs its motion to the propeller. A cutaway drawing, a diagram with part or the entire outer surface removed to expose the internal structure, can illustrate this mechanical complexity.

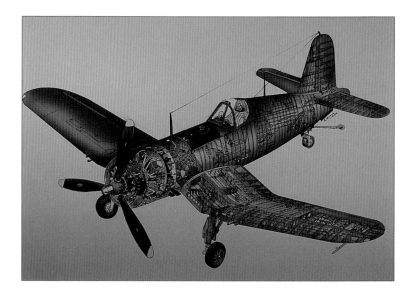

Cutaway drawings can be called skeletal renderings. Cutaways can be accomplished in black-and-white lines, monochrome, or full color. Although it may be helpful to draw from the actual object, cutaways are commonly drawn from blueprints, photographs, sketches, illustrated parts catalogues, or aircraft manufacturers' manuals.

The purpose of a cutaway is to depict internal structure and the machine's myriad parts. Cutaways of isolated systems are often used in technical manuals to show the interrelatedness of parts of a whole system. In aircraft, cutaways can illustrate the powerplant as well as the controls, hydraulics, fuel and oil, and the electrical systems. These

This cutaway drawing of the de Havilland DH-9 shows the internal wooden structural members in light brown and some key external parts—propeller, landing gear, wing struts, and tailskid—in a darker brown. Metal parts, including the engine, are depicted in gray. Note the wires and control cables. ©Andy Whyte, ASAA

drawings can be training aids, can illustrate manuals, can be used by mechanics involved in aircraft maintenance, or can simply be carefully constructed and precise works of art.

Cutaway drawings are sometimes used as advertising tools for aircraft sales. In addition to explanatory drawings of intricate systems, they demonstrate the interior design of the entire spectrum of business, military, and civilian aircraft.

An artist can tackle the precision of the cutaway to better understand and correctly paint the shape of an aircraft chosen as an art subject just as Rembrandt studied the skeleton of the human body to better depict his figures. An artist can draw cutaways for sales to magazines that cover aviation topics. Cutaways give you better insight into hardware and structure; the more knowledge obtained, the better the chance of success in depicting that subject. The information shown in cutaways is part of the basic knowledge of the machine that should be in an artist's mind before tackling a painting; it is another source to aid an artist in observation.

This cutaway drawing is of an advanced design, twin-rotor helicopter. It shows the engine position and some key structural members. ©Andy Whyte, ASAA

Like creating aircraft models to train an artist's knowledge of aircraft structure, studying, or, better yet, drawing cutaways can be a training exercise to an artist. In his biographical book on his aviation art, Keith Ferris wrote, "The structure of an aircraft very much affects the visual appearance of its external surface. An artist intent on showing texture and material, as well as the surface coating of an aircraft in his painting, finds strange undulations of the aircraft's skin as light is reflected from its surface. Structures also bend under load. Familiarity with structure explains these variations and allows a much more realistic painting."

↓ A scale side-view rendering of a Chance-Vought F4U Corsair. ©Andy Whyte, ASAA

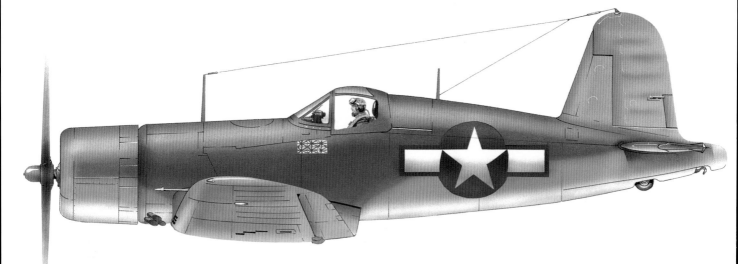

SCALE DRAWINGS

A scale drawing is another tool in the analysis and comprehension of the objects that you are trying to portray. Scale drawings are generally three views of an aircraft: flat reproductions of the top, bottom, and side. They are generally drawn for the purpose of illustrating the correct length, width, and height of an object and of all of its respective parts.

For aircraft modelers, scale refers to the size differential between the actual aircraft and the model aircraft. In 1:72 scale, popular with builders of model airplanes, the model is 72 times smaller than the actual aircraft.

↓ A scale side view of the Sikorsky UH-60D Night Hawk helicopter. ©Andy Whyte, ASAA

HH-60D NIGHT HAWK

COCKPITS AND INTERIORS

Drawing aircraft interiors is a challenge. Drawings range from depicting the rugged, battle-worn cockpit of a World War II Corsair to slick portrayals of a

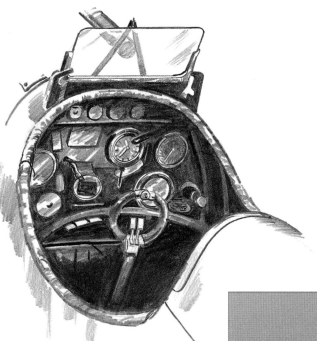

A pencil drawing of the open cockpit of a World War I SE-5 fighter. Note the ring-style control column or "stick" and the relatively few instruments. ©Andy Whyte, ASAA

In contrast to the relative simplicity of the SE-5, the interior of the futuristic glass cockpit shows the array of instruments and displays necessary to modern jets. ©Andy Whyte, ASAA

luxury business jet, designed to emphasize the beauty and comfort and to entice customers.

How do you draw cockpits and interiors? Focus on the subject and minimize the distractions that detract from your drawing. Every aircraft interior can be isolated and depicted—it's up to you, the artist, to determine *who* is your viewer, *why* you are making the drawing, and *what* you want to depict.

To draw interior scenes, enter the aircraft or sketch and photograph from a platform that allows a direct view of the cockpit.

Choose the view outward through the canopy or window as if your viewer is airborne.

Create as the center of interest the detail of the cockpit or gunner's position or center it outside of the craft. Consider differing views such as solo in an open cockpit biplane high over craggy mountains, with clouds and natural beauty seen through the glass canopy, as a passenger in an airliner high above the landscape below, or in a space shuttle as it docks with a space station.

Fly to add aerial scenes to your memory and to experience the emotions they elicit.

Sketch, draw, and photograph cockpits to determine their many differences and to learn well the cockpit you've chosen to portray.

Obtain the valuable reference materials—tech orders and aircraft manuals—that pertain to your particular aircraft. Check the library for books like *Cockpits*, by renowned photographer Dan Patterson, for artistic renderings of actual aircraft cockpits.

Determine the center of interest and use light and shadow to emphasize essentials.

Use three-point perspective to ensure correct perspective and proportions.

Allow the purpose of the drawing to dictate the amount of detail that is included.

Simplify. Everything in the area of the gunner's, the bombardier's, the navigator's, or the pilot's position does not have to be depicted.

↓ In this pencil drawing of a controller's console on an E-3A AWACS aircraft, the detail is indicated through the use of values. ©Andy Whyte, ASAA

What *is* depicted, however, should be accurately placed and, even if treated with subtlety, correct.

The interiors of airliners can be arranged as cargo carriers, crew transports, or for passengers. Research the differences between civilian and military aircraft—the Boeing 707, for example, and its counterparts, the U.S. Air Force E-3 AWACS, the KC-135 tankers, and Air Force One. There are vast differences in their interiors, one outfitted for passenger use, and the military versions with an entirely different purpose, mission, and interior design.

Note that the primary light source for the interior, although highly influenced by the light from the sun during daylight hours, will be cast

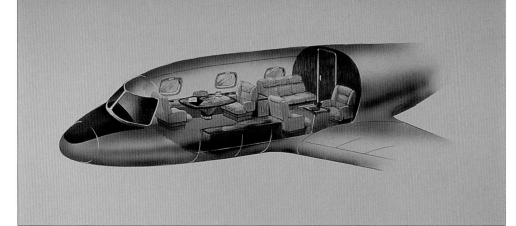

◄ Luxury is an important manufacturer's sales feature, as shown in an interior cabin design for a modern business aircraft. ©Andy Whyte, ASAA

by man-made lighting and diffused. Use the shadows to emphasize and define textures and surfaces. Put your shadows to work for you.

Note the similarities and the differences in the layout and instrumentation of civilian general aviation aircraft, civil airliners, and military aircraft. Work at learning to draw the head's-up display (HUD) on the fighter cockpit canopy. Use techniques of drawing like crosshatching, shading, and rubbing to show texture and materials in carpeted and upholstered interiors in business and executive aircraft.

When you add color to your drawings, study camouflage schemes for external portions of aircraft. Know that even those military aircraft that are bare metal will generally be grimy and oil-streaked in a wartime situation. Some will have altered colors, for example the P-40s that were painted a tan that faded to pink in hot desert sunshine. Although there is a preponderance of olive drab and gray in crafts like the C-130 Hercules, there are many variations in the shades of green and gray. Whether working on an interior or exterior image, study the perspective and proportions.

↑ Another interior cabin design for an executive aircraft that focuses on a high degree of comfort and modern business communications equipment. ©Andy Whyte, ASAA

Precision and Creativity

Walter Matthews Jefferies

Cutaway drawings and scale views, aviation art forms that have been among the hallmarks of Walter "Matt" Jefferies' work for over 50 years, require the utmost in painstaking research and accuracy. They are as precise as engineering drawings and blueprints, yet they can be as creative as paintings.

Noting two key facts for artists who would work in these demanding forms, he explained, "Dimensions on factory prints and in an aircraft manual (Technical Order, or T.O.) will be in inches, not feet and inches. The most valuable manuals to use as reference for drawing aircraft to scale are (1) the Erection and Maintenance Manual, (2) the Overhaul and Structural Repair Manual, and (3) the Illustrated Parts Catalogue. The latter is absolutely necessary for inboard profiles and cutaways."

The cutaway drawings of the F-86A and the P-47D are excellent examples of the precision of Jefferies' work, as is the Grumman F9F-8 Cougar, first flown in 1955 by the U.S. Navy's Aerial Demonstration Team, the Blue Angels. His two-page magazine layout of the U.S. Jet Air Force, done in 1956, provides another look at the research and drafting skills of Jefferies. Note the powerplant and armament data provided and that each grid square equals 5 feet.

Jefferies' precision has carried over into his creative work on canvas and as a television and motion picture art director. The scale drawing of his design, the starship *Enterprise* that he originated for *Star Trek*, exemplifies his creativity. Truly, Matt's has been a long, distinguished, and varied career.

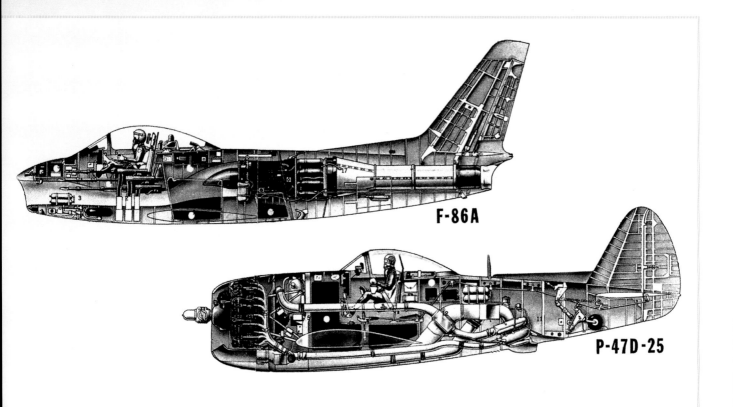

Two more of Jefferies' cutaway drawings: a North American F-86A Sabre and a Republic P-47D Thunderbolt. Both highlight the detail within the fuselages of the two aircraft.
©Walter Matthews Jeffries

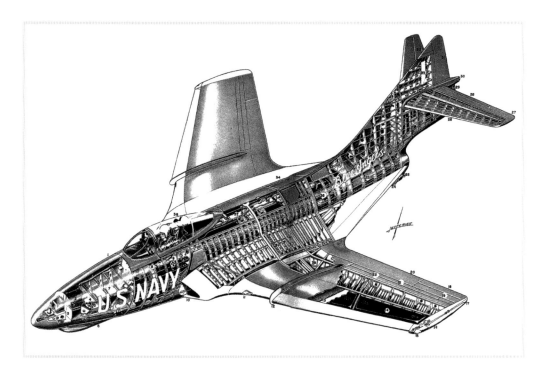

Depicting a great deal of the structural detail, a
U.S. Navy Blue Angel's Grumman F9F-8 Cougar is
drawn as a perspective cutaway by Jefferies.
©*Walter Matthews Jeffries*

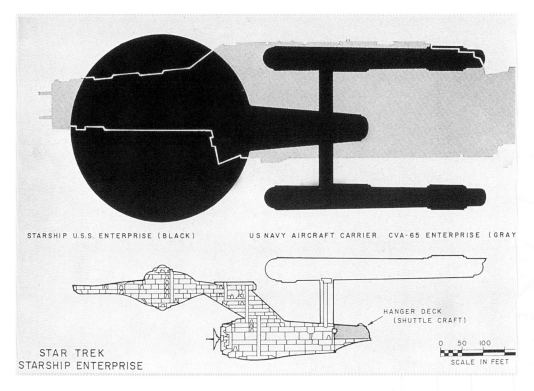

A scale drawing of Matt Jeffries' original design of
the starship *Enterprise*. ©*Walter Matthews Jeffries*

n aviation art, cartoons can be used to advertise, to educate, to caution about safety, to amuse, and/or to poke fun at aviators and aviation." Andy Whyte, ASAA

CARTOONS AND

AEROCATURES™

In the mid-1700s, a cartoon was an artist's initial drawing to develop a painting, mosaic, fresco, or tapestry. The cartoon was preliminary to the creation of a work of art. Within a hundred years and with the coming of political satire and caricatures that emphasized the outstanding features of well-known figures, the cartoon came to refer to pictorial humor. A cartoon became a visual statement found in editorial sections of newspapers and magazines. Over time, a cartoon became a mockery and a form of public ridicule—a captioned or uncaptioned humorous drawing. In the modern use of the term, a cartoon, and collections of printed cartoons in a series, became the art form for animated films and comic strips.

➤ Dot Swain Lewis' cartoon of a World War II member of the Women Airforce Service Pilots, a WASP, on the Flight Line at Sweetwater, Texas' Avenger Field, is complete with oxygen mask and chest-pack parachute.

A cartoon is a single drawing or a series of drawings that makes a point or tells a joke or story about subjects such as human activities, fads, fashions, sports, and political and historical events. In aviation art, cartoons can be used to advertise, educate, caution about safety, amuse, and poke fun at aviators and aviation. Cartoons often exaggerate, but differ from caricatures that distort figures and emphasize certain features or peculiarities. Cartoons can be captioned or can contain dialogue. Cartoons can be anthropomorphic, ascribing human characteristics to animals or machines, with the intention of making a point, attracting attention, or motivating, informing, and, above all, amusing.

Cartoons were introduced to the public through the printed page. By the nineteenth and twentieth centuries, cartoons were established as legitimate forms of commentary. During the early 1800s, lithography eased the cost and availability of reproduced

↑ Designed for male pilots, the WASP flying suits, as depicted in another Dot Lewis cartoon, came in only one size—large!

↓ Parachute Systems, Inc. commissioned Hank Caruso to portray aerobatic aircraft by Butler. For *"The Art of Aero-Knot-ics"*, Caruso was challenged to develop the story he wanted to tell and with the complexity of the geometry and physics. Searching for a dynamic pose, he opted to have four aerobatic aircraft tie a smoke knot, a play on words for his title. The dynamic scene involved each with extreme maneuvers, yet out of one another's way. Caruso's preliminary sketch concentrated on the drawing of the smoke knot. With the aircraft flying toward the viewer, an exaggerated perspective was needed and the geometry made it possible for each aircraft to warily eye the other.

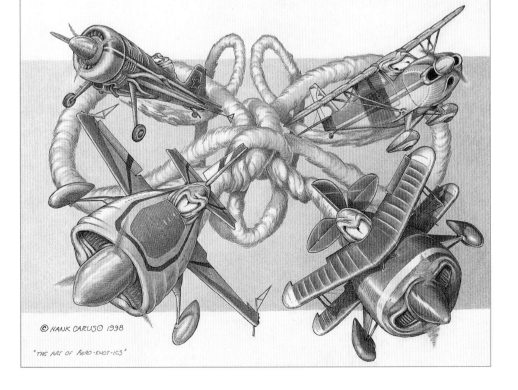

© HANK CARUSO 1998

"THE ART OF AERO-KNOT-ICS"

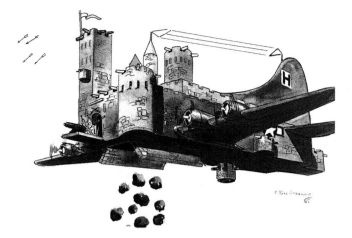

Courtesy of the United States Air Force Museum in Dayton, Ohio, these four World War II cartoons are C. Ross Greening's caricatures of well-known aircraft of the era.

Col. C. Ross Greening was one of Jimmy Doolittle's Tokyo Raiders and later a German Prisoner of War. As a morale booster, he taught art to other POWs at Stalag Luft One.

⬇ P-47 *Thunderbolt*, the "Jug"

⬆ B-17 *Flying Fortress*

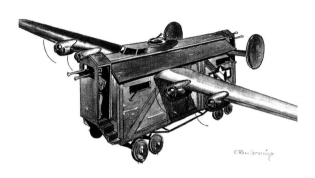

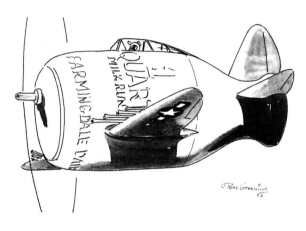

⬆ B-24 *Liberator*

drawings; cartoons and caricatures became more widespread. In the twentieth century, cartoonists like Thomas Nast, Milton Caniff, and Bill Mauldin became famous. Drawing attention to U.S. fighting forces, Caniff drew "Mail Call" for Camp Newspaper Service, popularized "Terry and the Pirates" during the war, and started "Steve Canyon" at the end of the war. Mauldin, a sergeant, was a combat cartoonist who drew two main characters, "Willie and Joe," a pair of combat infantrymen. In 1945, Mauldin's cartoons on World War II won the Pulitzer Prize. He was quoted as having said, "I drew pictures for and about the soldiers because I knew what their life was like and understood their gripes. I wanted to make something out of the humorous situations that come up even when you don't think life could be any more miserable."

Fifty-five years later, as the year 2000 began, the G.I. that was popularized by Mauldin's Willie and Joe, was named by *TIME* magazine as the "Most Influential Person of the Century." Illustrating the "female G.I.," Dorothy Swain Lewis created cartoon illustrations of the Women's Airforce Service Pilots (WASP) for the first book published about the WASP immediately after World War II. Her cartoons were also featured in her biography, *How High She Flies*.

CARICATURE

Caricature generally is based on an easily identifiable person with distortion or enlargement to a particular characteristic. Some of the best-known caricaturists drew pictures that emphasized particular physical or facial features, dress, or manners to create a ridiculous effect. They were directed at individuals, at political, religious, and social situations or institutions, and/or at actions by various groups of society.

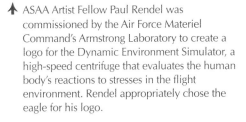

In aviation, caricature of a particular aviator might focus on a distinguishing trait or characteristic. Perhaps an air racer like flamboyant Roscoe Turner with his pet lion named Gilmore could inspire a caricature. Aviatrix Harriet Quimby, eye-catching in her purple satin flying outfit, could be depicted in her Bleriot, the first woman to fly solo across the English Channel. Her triumph gained little notice as she landed in France the evening before the great ship *Titanic* lost its battle with an iceberg.

To create a caricature of a person or aircraft requires a close observation of the subject, and, when it is an aircraft, an intimate knowledge of its form and its respective parts, before one can distort its outstanding or unique features. Perhaps in choosing a unique focal point of the Fairchild Republic A-10, one might exaggerate the deadly General Electric Avenger 30-mm seven-barrel cannon mounted on the nose. One might depict the F4U Corsair on a carrier, its unique gull-shaped wings folded over its canopy; the Super Guppy, its enlarged fuselage ballooning over the cockpit; or the Cobra helicopter, its very name inspiring ideas for an artist.

STUDY SUCCESSFUL CARICATURISTS

If you are interested in cartoons or caricatures, study the works of the highly successful Hank Caruso. Look, learn, and laugh; but recognize the studious research, knowledge, and dedication to precision that underlies each Caruso *Aerocature*™. Remember—there are no shortcuts! Learn to draw. Research your subject and free your imagination to create cartoons and caricatures. Then draw, draw, and draw.

ASAA Artist Fellow Paul Rendel was commissioned by the Air Force Materiel Command's Armstrong Laboratory to create a logo for the Dynamic Environment Simulator, a high-speed centrifuge that evaluates the human body's reactions to stresses in the flight environment. Rendel appropriately chose the eagle for his logo.

Four final Space Shuttle Mission patches were created by Mark Pestana. Note the individual characteristics of each mission as well as the names of the crewmembers.

↟ STS–93

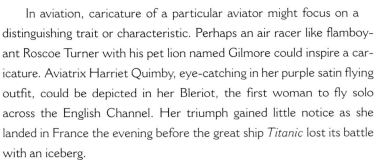

↟ STS–89

↟ STS–69

↟ STS–86

How to Draw *Aerocatures*™

Hank Caruso, ASAA

Outstanding caricaturist Hank Caruso has established a unique niche in aviation art. His *Aerocatures*™ are drawings that exaggerate and highlight identifiable aspects of the aircraft of his choice. Caruso said: "I regard cartoons as the punch line and caricatures as the story. Caricatures are drawings that are based on reality: real people, real stories, real objects. I view my art as portraits of how man-made objects, physical forces, and human feelings come together and interact. In selecting the most important aspects of particular aircraft, each drawing involves considerable research, observation, and insight."

Thunderflushed/Thunderstuck
Because fighter aircraft were more limited in range than the bombers they protected, an experimental program sought to modify B-36 bombers to carry RF-84F Thunderflash and F-84F Thunderstreak fighters with them into combat. Hank Caruso worked out solutions to visual problems in his preliminary sketch, focusing on composition, shapes, viewing angle, props, expressions, lighting, and contours, and ignoring "extra" lines and uncorrected "mistakes." His shading densities along the aircraft fuselages suggest reflections on bare metal surfaces, emphasize the curvature of airplane surfaces, and represent shadows to separate the aircraft from the cloud background. Caruso said, "Notice how black-and-white lines are able to suggest the same visual ideas that are provided by color." *©Hank Caruso*

Caruso addresses eight specific issues: story, anatomy, geometry, physics, pose, lighting, surface and contour, and props. He advises, "Have a clear vision of the story that you want to tell. If the story simply is an airplane portrait, choose the aspect of its character that you want to emphasize—perhaps its speed, size, use, or lethality."

In creating either a caricature *or* a serious rendering, he suggests, "Have a thorough understanding of the aircraft's anatomy and operating features. Be sure to research unique design and construction aspects, being aware, for example, that the left side of the fuselage might differ from the right. Accuracy is important."

Caruso said, "Decide how you will position the aircraft and other elements in your drawing, choosing where the viewer will be positioned with respect to them. Proper perspective is critical to the correct geometry."

The physics of the situation is important, although it may not be obvious. "Any depiction of an aircraft should be appropriate for its maneuver," said Caruso. "If you fail to consider the proper bank angle, the forces of gravity and lift, or make other subtle violations of the laws of physics, the picture might not 'look right' to the viewer even if he or she can't describe why."

Pose the craft appropriately and ensure that the lighting enhances the story that you're telling. Caruso added, "Where is the light coming from? Will significant areas of the craft be in shadow so that shape rather than detail is important? Is the lighting directional or diffuse? Is it consistent for all of the elements of the drawing?"

When focusing on surface and contour, Caruso explained, "Capturing the differences in surface types and subtle variations in contour can make a drawing much more accurate and interesting. Ask yourself, 'Which surfaces are reflective and which are not? If the drawing is black and white, how can different types of shading suggest different surface types and paint colors? Do rounded surfaces show up as round or flat? Are complex, but characteristic, surface contours accurately depicted?'"

In his award-winning style, Caruso imaginatively selects props that enhance his drawings and add emphasis to the caricature that he is depicting. His choices of props complete the picture and give it interest. He said: "Props may provide important information needed to understand the story. Too few and the story may not be apparent. Too many and the picture might be cluttered and confusing. Make sure that the props selected are appropriate for the operational conditions and time period. Be subtle. Prominent props compete for attention with the picture and the story elements."

Hank Caruso uses pen and ink. He said: "I particularly like the degree of control over each line that pen and ink gives me. I'm fascinated that simple lines can create the impression of contour and suggest a variety of different surface types (wood, water, clouds, metal). As an aerospace test engineer, I started with and continue to use Rapidograph drafting pens. I use the finest point when I begin inking, in case I make a mistake or change my mind. The thin ink line is relatively easy to remove with a sharp razorblade.

"As much as I like black-and-white line images, the picture comes alive with color and I use Prismacolor colored pencils directly on the black-and-white rendering. I like the close control of the colors and the way colors can be overlaid and blended to create smooth tonal changes that are unlike most people's expectations of a pencil rendering."

Using a hard, smooth surface, Caruso works on a pad of smooth, Strathmore or Bienfang 100-pound Bristol. He admitted, "The main drawback to working in ink and colored pencil is that it is time-consuming to fill a large space. My originals typically range from 11 inches by 14 inches to 19 inches by 24 inches."

He starts with felt-tip pen sketches. "I don't work from photographs or models when I begin to sketch. I believe that, if I can't create an effective preliminary drawing 'out of my head,' I probably don't understand my subject well enough." For correct detail, he uses numerous reference materials later. Caruso believes that an initial drawing from reference materials results in bad copies of photographs and that they lack life and originality."

Hank Caruso's unique *Aerocatures*™, whether black-and-white or color, fill a special niche in aviation art. His methods are worthy of careful study.

LIGHT AND SHADOW

Know the Light Source—Keep It Consistent

"If a square is painted black and white and illuminated with an obvious light source, the white section in the shadow will be a lower (darker) value than the black section with the light on it. I try to keep this in mind." *Andy Whyte, ASAA*

A light source, reflected light, shadow, and values are basic to drawing and painting. A value is created *because* of light. The angle at which light strikes a surface determines the relative degree of lightness or shadow to the form. The more direct the light source, the lower or whiter the value; that is, a surface that is 90 degrees to the light source receives more light than a surface that is at a 45-degree angle.

VALUES

Remember that values—the lightness or the darkness of the objects that compose a drawing or a painting—determine the relationships between compositional elements (see chapter 4). Everything in art is relative. An object painted in one particular value can look light or dark depending upon its surroundings. It may be easier to think of values in shades of gray—if you mix a small bit of black with a lot of white, the result will be a very high value. The greater the amount of black, the lower the value.

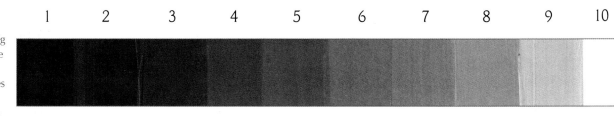

1 2 3 4 5 6 7 8 9 10

➤ Revisiting the value scale of 10 values ranging from the darkest dark—black—at a value of 1 to the lightest light—white—at a value of 10. Values set a mood and play an important role in composition and design. ©Andy Whyte, ASAA

Values play an important part in composition and design. Values set a mood.

The way we see is dependent upon the amount of light on a subject. Highlights will be brighter and shadows darker on clear, sunny days. The effects of atmospheric distance and reduced light will bring values closer together—highlights will be reduced and shadows will be

➤ An object drawn in a particular value can appear lighter or darker depending on its surroundings. The gray square in the center of the larger squares is the same value in all four. It appears darker when surrounded by a lighter value and lighter when surrounded by a darker one. ©Andy Whyte, ASAA

lighter. There are a number of factors in creating the illusion of depth in a painting: perspective, overlapping of objects, using hard and soft edges, reducing detail, changing value, and intensity of color. Divide the painting into three areas: foreground, middle ground, and background.

When light values dominate, as in a high-key drawing, the contrast between highlights and shadows helps to define the shape of the aircraft more clearly. On a clear, sunny day, highlights will be brighter and shadows will be darker.

LIGHT SOURCE AND REFLECTED LIGHT

To draw objects that are on the surface of the earth, an artist chooses his or her natural light source and establishes the natural horizon. The artist depicts the source of the light—above, behind, beside, or in front of the object. To draw aircraft, the third dimension of height complicates that compositional challenge. The aircraft's location and its angle of attack and attitude relative to the horizon might place the natural light *beneath* the craft. Aircraft, with their various shapes, cast interesting shadows that tend to be fluid. The cast shadow will be as aerodynamically sleek as are the parts of the aircraft. Depending upon the materials composing the aircraft and/or a painted or highly reflective surface, there is reflected light to take into consideration. Remember that once you have selected the source of the natural light, it is imperative to remain consistent throughout the scene.

◀ This painting demonstrates the factors involved in creating the illusion of depth. The foreground, middle ground, and background are established through the use of perspective, overlapping objects, soft and hard edges, reduced detail, changing values, and intensity of color. ©Andy Whyte, ASAA

▼ The lesser range of values shows the effects of reduced light and atmospheric distance on this same F-86 Sabre. ©Andy Whyte, ASAA

◀ Our ability to see an object clearly is dependent upon the amount of light on that object. In bright light, there is a greater range of values. ©Andy Whyte, ASAA

DIRECT LIGHT AND CHIAROSCURO

Chiaroscuro (key-ah-ro-SKEW-ro), the use of light and shadow in drawing or painting, is necessary to the creation of the illusion of depth, form, and distance and to provide dramatic effects. An artist uses chiaroscuro, which hinges upon the selection of the light source and the intensity and angle of that light, to create subtle gradations in value and distinct variations of light and shade.

Direct lighting—from the sun, the moon, a flash of lightning, or from a manufactured light source—outlines and shapes an object, gives it form. To give three-dimensional shape to an object on your paper or canvas, select that light source. By temporarily sketching a series of geometric figures, note the places on the shapes that would take the direct light and reflect a highlight, the pinpoint of the direct light source. Note the portions that are bathed in more subdued light and determine the side of each object that is in shadow, identifying a core shadow that is the center of the darkened side. Notice that, on that darkened side, some light is reflected from another area or from a secondary light source. This lighter area on the dark side is essential in creating the three-dimensional form on your paper or canvas. The object itself casts a shadow and that cast shadow is essential in creating space for the image.

Lighting can:

- Define unique features of a particular aircraft.
- Set a mood.
- Establish the time of day—the low light of twilight or high intensity of midday.
- Cast long, intriguing shadows, create interesting shapes, and create drama.
- Emphasize a scene's areas of interest and effectively lead the eye of the viewer throughout the drawing.
- Bring a drawing into balance with either several gradual value changes or with a few sharply contrasting values.
- Create interest with a subtlety that emphasizes a particular form even when that form is in a darkened portion of the drawing.

↑ This drawing of three geometric shapes shows the use of direct light and shadows in creating three dimensions on a flat surface. Note that both the objects themselves and the cast shadows exhibit a range of values. ©Andy Whyte, ASAA

REFLECTED LIGHT

Light is absorbed, scattered, or reflected in passing through the atmosphere. Reflected light, a secondary light source, is useful to an artist in creating the remainder of a form. Reflected light helps to define the back shape of an object, the area in shadow. It is important to remember that lighting outdoors always has a reflected light source.

One more consideration is the shape of reflections on rounded surfaces, as many aircraft surfaces are not only curved, but also highly reflective. The more highly curved the surface, the more curved an object's reflection will become. A reflection is being shown from the artist's or viewer's standpoint. Note that the intensity is diminished in a reflection, as is rigidity of a form.

Be consistent once you have decided upon the time of day and the primary light source for your drawing. The angle of the natural light is the artist's to determine, but a composition fails quickly when light and shadow seem to come from different locations in one scene.

INDIRECT LIGHT AND SHADOW

Because what you are drawing is light, the darker portions of your scene are indirectly lit and take on lower values. Second and even third light sources are caused by reflection and other light sources that are present in the environment. In the absence of light, the transition to darker values is sudden. A shadow is solidly black when there is *no* light. In a drawing or painting, there must be some source of illumination. Even the most shadowed portion of a form must have enough ambient light to make that form visible or completed in the eye of the viewer.

Shadows can:

- Accentuate the light and create a heightened interest in areas of light.
- Offer a balance to a composition.
- Provide the negative space to balance areas of positive space.
- Give a space for items of relatively less interest in a composition, yet that more fully describe and complete the scene.
- Create more intensity in the light by contrast.
- Create velocity and motion.
- Be contrived rather than natural for emphasis.

Shadows differ depending upon the light source. Rays of light from a manufactured source—flashlight, headlight, overhead light, or spotlight—radiate in all directions. The sun's rays radiate also, but are from so much greater a distance that they tend to act in parallel lines rather than spreading like a fan from a single source.

Cast shadows, like positive forms, have a separate system of values. The darkest dark will be found in the portion of the cast shadow that is closest to the object casting the shadow. The lightest light will be at the edge of the shadow.

Shadows have perspective. If the light source is directly above an object, the cast shadows go in every direction. When the light source is

Quote

"It is important to balance lights and darks, areas of light and shadow."

↑ This is a "high key" painting, limited to the higher values of the colors. This F4U Corsair is bathed in bright sunlight; it tends to look washed out. ©Andy Whyte, ASAA

↑ In contrast, this "low key" painting utilizes the lower values. The darker tones throughout suggest a night scene. ©Andy Whyte, ASAA

→ This painting uses a full range of values—from the darkest dark to the lightest light. Note the dark shadow beneath the airplane and the higher values of the trees receding into the distance. ©Andy Whyte, ASAA

the sun or the moon, the vanishing point for the perspective of the shadow is on the horizon directly below the light source.

Backlighting, although it mutes the detail, color, and form of the craft, can heighten interest in an aircraft and create drama. Backlighting creates shadow and reflected light as the light source for the form closest to the viewer.

Use the shadows of clouds to create depth in atmospheric perspective. Use the shadows of mountain peaks to accentuate the ruggedness of the terrain. Use shadows flitting across still water to create interest in the surface of a lake or pond. Use the shadow of the airborne aircraft, distorted on the waves of the ocean, to give height to the waves and to create atmospheric distance between the aircraft and the water.

It is important to balance lights and darks, areas of light and shadow. As you practice with quickly sketched thumbnails to develop good compositions, remember to develop good proportions between light and shadow. Work to create a good scheme for a balance of lights and darks.

Depicting Depth, Form, and Distance

Sharon Rajnus

Sharon Rajnus (*Rye-nuss*) was an artist prior to becoming a pilot in the 1970s. Her certificate still relatively new, she joined her husband, Don, for an invaluable hands-on learning experience. They worked with an Airframe and Powerplant Mechanic (A&P) to rebuild a 1948 Stinson 108-2. When that "taildragger" had been completed and certified, they flew to Alaska to amass a lifetime of experience in one adventurous summer. Sharon said, "We witnessed gorgeous country and breathtaking skies—sunrises and sunsets, clouds, rain, and brilliant sunshine."

The aerial odyssey carried Sharon and Don over the rugged land in which most of the United States' 75,000 square kilometers of glaciers are located. Sharon couldn't help but be inspired by these immense rivers of ice. She witnessed the incredible calving that transformed a huge segment of ice into an iceberg in a thunderous, cracking, splashing birth. As glacial ice absorbs all other colors and reflects the sky and water that surround it, she saw dramatic blues—from cobalt to ultramarine to azure—and values that were the darkest dark in the deep cavities and lightest light where the ice was spotlighted by the sun—the light and shadow that glaciers seemed to embody.

"Aircraft are out of their element on the ground," said Sharon. "In paintings, I choose to show the *sense* of flight, the *feel* of the air."

Inspired to create a series of glacier paintings, she includes the colors of snow that have been compressed into ice that has carved, wedged, plucked, and abraded its way to valleys, cirques, and the sea. She emphasizes the blues that are reflected by that ice and the variety of light and shadow that plays across the landscape and creates depth, form, and distance in painting.

If you select backgrounds of natural beauty like glaciers, mountains, seashores, or sculpted desert sandstone, try to visit such environments to *know* your subject. Know what you paint.

Glacier Flying—OS2U Kingfisher
**The OS2U Kingfisher was used extensively in the Alaskan theater during World War II, principally for observation and scouting, but also for air-sea rescue or armed with two 100-pound bombs. Able to be fitted with fixed-wheel landing gear or floats, the Kingfisher could be operated on land or, float-equipped, by landing alongside a carrier and winched aboard. ©*Sharon Rajnus*

Meeting the Challenge

William S. "Bill" Phillips, ASAA

A wingman is a pilot whose plane is positioned behind a lead pilot in a tight formation. In his evocative and memorable works of art, William S. "Bill" Phillips has often shown us the wingman's view. Phillips takes us into the action and exhilaration of flight by keeping us poised in tight formation, flinging ourselves in air as does the aircraft that has commanded our complete attention.

Although he had always enjoyed drawing and aircraft, when Phillips chose an art career he imposed a three-year vigorous program of self-study. "From the library, which is full of art information, I read every book on art that I could find. Once I had mastered the texts, I kept advancing. I worked at drawing, at painting, and to this day I continue to learn."

Obtaining actual flights with experienced pilots is his research platform. He said: "I use a lot of videos for the continuum of rapid action. Single-frame photos freeze the time and leave no hint as to what continues to happen. In addition to enhancing my memory, film allows me to see again the ground blur, the changing light, and the movement of control surfaces and other aircraft. When I commit a scene to canvas, I don't want a static scene of a flying airplane."

Phillips likes to believe that his art moves beyond what a camera can capture. He said, "With a certain amount of fantasy in the piece, I want the scene to be something neither I nor anyone else has ever seen."

He is an avid participant in the Air Force Art Program, which has charged artists to produce fine art: graphic depictions of missions, locations, equipment, aircraft, crew members, and the ongoing history of the U.S. Air Force. As a Navy combat artist in 1988, viewing naval operations in the Persian Gulf, Phillips worked from 10 different ships. While aboard a cruiser that pulled aft of a carrier, he started snapping photographs. In creating a painting of the scene, the angle of the carrier, the background sunset, and the setting sun's reflection on the water were of his own dramatic imagination and creation.

Home Is the Hunter ©William S. Phillips

Phillips said: "Fundamental to aviation art is the chance to contribute a unique perspective to the ancient disciplines of art, for never before has the artist been allowed to place his subject in a painting with such vast distances between subject and background. Never has there been the opportunity to glimpse the earth with its wealth of form and light from this vantage point. There is a challenge to the artist when confronted by flight and its unique opportunities to involve the viewer in a world of grace and fluid motion—a world many people will never experience. The realm of high-performance flight is combined with history and rare beauty."

Phillips generally begins his involvement in a scene with a static aircraft walk-around. When airborne, he analyzes light and dark, cloud shadows on the earth, airplane shadows on the clouds, reflections, and the blurring of colors and shapes in motion.

Most of Phillips' paintings start as abstracts. He works to develop a successful combination of form and design. "I analyze where darks and lights should be, how the work comes together best, attention to the line, and a pleasing composition. From there I work it up to decide where the airplane will go to enhance that design."

Bill Phillips pushes his artistic envelope. He continues to draw; he continues to paint. He challenges himself to do his best; then he strives to meet and surpass that challenge.

Lear over Crater Lake ©William S. Phillips

COMPOSITION

Make a Whole More than the Sum of Its Parts

"A n artistic composition is a spatial relationship that creates an aesthetically pleasing picture and gives the illusion of three dimensions on a two-dimensional surface." *Andy Whyte, ASAA*

So far in this book we've talked about knowledge of aircraft, how they fly, and some special considerations in drawing them; we have looked at the tools available for drawing, and have discussed sketching and line drawing. Research methods—and some dangers—have been addressed, as has linear perspective, the ways of representing three-dimensional objects on two-dimensional surfaces. Some specialized types of drawing—cutaways, scale views, aircraft interiors and cockpits, cartoons and caricatures—have been described and attention has focused on light and shadow and the importance of values in drawing—the darkest darks, lightest lights, and the full range of gradations between. Now it is time to start to bring these elements together into an artistic composition, to compose a completed drawing involving an aircraft. With a basis in fundamental principles, composition is the transforming of the raw material of a good idea into an original artwork.

Reduced to simple terms, a composition is an image formed by a series of lines, shapes, values, and colors. Throughout the years, many talented artists and teachers have described and discussed the fundamental principles of composition and all have contributed to our knowledge and understanding. We give special credit to aviation artist Robert Watts for his application of those principles in compositions. Here are some basics to help you create a composition.

GOOD IDEAS

Begin with a good idea, one that has captured your attention and that inspires the best artistic work possible. The idea can be a portrait of a new aircraft, it can be a historic or current moment, or it can be an imaginative scene that you are inspired to draw. The possibilities are limited only by your imagination and willingness to work. A good idea is usually one that an artist knows will appeal to an audience and, if appropriate, one that will meet a client's requirements. This book is filled with the expression of good ideas; they should provide a wide range of inspiration. We believe that the natural and manufactured world around us, with its constant change, is the primary source of good ideas.

WELL PRESENTED, WELL DRAWN

Even the best of ideas poorly expressed will fail to capture viewers. There is no substitute for drawing well. It takes hard work

With a simple subject, like this F-86 Sabre, a more complicated background would work. Using differing values will focus attention on the prominent object. ©Andy Whyte, ASAA

and lots of practice. If the idea—or subject—is a simple one, like a single aircraft, a more complex setting will be appropriate. If the subject is complex, with multiple aircraft, then a simple background will work best.

Aircraft, like actors, have a "best side." That is, their key character-istics are best seen from a particular point of view. On the next page are two examples of military fighters with distinct wing configurations.

IN A BALANCED WAY

Your job is to create a composition that brings the viewers' eyes into the scene, to circulate them from the main focal point of the art-work to subordinate points, and to return to the work's main focal

A complex subject would work best with a simple background. Andy Whyte prefers "to keep the aircraft reasonably tight, to focus on it as the main subject. In a semirealistic way, I like the background, which should be easily identified, to be indistinct and not highly detailed. The background should not detract from the subject." ©Andy Whyte, ASAA

← The outstanding and easily identifiable characteristic of the F4U Corsair is its unique wing, named for the shape of the seagull wing that inspired its design. This gullwing F4U Corsair is not showing its "best side" to advantage. ©Andy Whyte, ASAA

◄Highlighting the negative and positive dihedral of the F4U wing is a better compositional choice. Here the characteristic gullwing is apparent and the aircraft is easily recognizable. ©Andy Whyte, ASAA

← Choose a shape that enhances the dominant object to the best advantage. Here the graceful slant of the F-86 Sabre jet is only partially shown. Even if the linear perspective is correct, this doesn't "look right" to a viewer. ©Andy Whyte, ASAA

← Showing its "best side," the characteristic sweptwing adds interest to the composition and is more convincing. ©Andy Whyte, ASAA

point. Four models for composing drawings that are balanced on the drawing surface and that move the viewer's eye around the complete subject matter, beginning with the dominant subject, are:

- Divide the space into quadrants in which values change from light in one quadrant, to a darker value in the second, still darker in the third, and very dark in the fourth.
- Divide the space sequentially with changing sizes and changing values in an asymmetrical manner.
- Create a dynamic balance between two sides of your paper, between negative and positive forms. With the repetition of an element—one shape, one color, and one line—objects can be connected visually.
- Use the Golden Mean. With a specific mathematical equation as its basis, it has been used for composition in architecture, mathematics, poetry, music, and art. (See Andy Whyte's sidebar in this chapter.)

For aviation art, the placement of the horizon—the eye level of the viewer—is a key consideration. Because flying provides an opportunity to view objects on the surface of the earth in a new way, it is vital that the horizon be consistent within the work of art. There are some key rules relating to the placement of the horizon and to the placement of objects with respect to it. Among them are:

- Do not place the horizon line in the center of the drawing.
- Do not position an aircraft on the horizon line.
- Do not place your dominant object directly in the center of your drawing.

An effective aviation art composition will require a dominant figure, other subdominant figures, and one or more different or discordant figures. A single fighter aircraft with a somewhat smaller "wingman" and an enemy shown above a simple landscape, made somewhat indistinct through aerial perspective, is but one example. There are many others available to you throughout this book.

Look to establish a balance throughout the composition. Lines define shapes. You are the artist who determines whether they will be faint or bold, straight or curved. Lines can be horizontal, vertical, or on the diagonal. The choice of those directions is

↓This torpedo bomber is "perched" directly on the horizon line—a compositional error to be avoided. Place your objects above or below the horizon and avoid having the object and the horizon exactly parallel to one another. ©Andy Whyte, ASAA

up to you. A diagonal line can convey movement and speed. A horizontal line can convey mood and emotion. A vertical line can convey strength. By repetition, the weights and shapes of your lines can unite portions of the drawing that would otherwise be disconnected in your drawing.

ACCURATE AND CONSISTENT

Much of aviation art is representational. It seeks to present an image of something that exists—or has existed in the past—in the man-made or natural world. If your drawings are to be representational and not impressionistic or abstract, they must be accurate and, within the drawing, consistent. Accuracy requires careful research into the scene or objects to be presented and proper perspective in the presentation. Be consistent with the sources of light—direct and reflected. Be consistent, too, with the horizon; it should not evenly divide your drawing surface.

This doesn't mean that there is little room for artistic creativity in aviation art. Nothing could be further from the truth. The imagination of the artist is of vital importance in the good ideas chosen and in their balanced presentation. If, however, facts are being presented, they must be presented accurately and consistently. Viewers of aviation art tend to be knowledgeable and precise; if they find a flaw in a drawing, their attention will be lost and the objective of the drawing will be missed.

A FULL RANGE OF VALUES

An effective drawing uses a full range of values for several reasons. The full range adds balance to the drawing and serves to move the viewer's eye throughout it. Using that full range—from darkest darks, which tend to recede, through the full range to lightest lights, which advance in a drawing—also helps to create the illusion of depth and enhances the establishment of a foreground, middle ground, and background. Values will help the artist direct the attention of the viewer to the dominant, subdominant, and lesser shapes that make up the complete drawing.

Knowledge of values and of the impact of the surroundings on those values helps the artist create tonal plans for the drawings to be done. Here are four examples of tonal plan development.

Developing your tonal plans—how you plan to utilize the range of values—will require your thoughtful consideration of time of day, weather, and the source(s) of light as well as your compositional planning for your subject. Dramatic lighting will enhance your composition and your drawing.

Quote

"A good composition begins with a good idea, well presented and well drawn, in a balanced way."
Robert Watts, ASAA

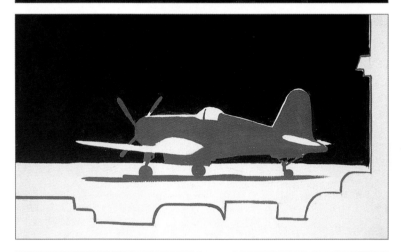

Drawings like these enable the development of a tonal plan for a drawing and assist in using a full range of values in the foreground, middle ground, and background. In general terms, low values would be used in the dark sector, middle values in the sector shown in gray, and high values in the white area. Value drawings can give you practice in creating good compositions. Tonal drawings help you become consistent with the placement of objects in relation to the horizon in respect to the light source, its resultant shadows, and reflections. ©Andy Whyte, ASAA

➤ In this daylight scene, the darkest darks or lowest values are in the shadowed foreground, the aircraft is in the middle ground. ©Andy Whyte, ASAA

◄ In this night scene with a dark sky, a lower-key drawing, the middle and foreground are lighted. Note the higher values on the wings, canopy, upper fuselage, and tail surfaces. ©Andy Whyte, ASAA

◄ In this composition, a daylight scene, the middle ground is in dark shadow. ©Andy Whyte, ASAA

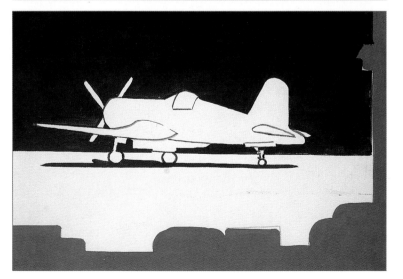

◄ Another night scene, fully lighted in the middle ground and with midrange values in the foreground. ©Andy Whyte, ASAA

Putting the Picture Together

Robert Watts, ASAA

Note Robert Watts' mastery of creating a foreground, middle ground, and background in his paintings. Note, too, his successful use of dominant, subdominant, and sub-subdominant objects in *Dicing the Wall* which depicts a P-38 Lighting partrolling German defensive fortifications.

"If you don't know how to draw like gangbusters, you'd better get hot on that project. There is no substitute for good drawing!" Robert Watts, ASAA

On solving the composition, Robert Watts said, "Planning—the muscle in your brain gets stronger as you use it. . . . Look into every aspect of your proposed painting. . . . It never ceases to amaze me what can go wrong with a composition. It is part of the mystical process. The fatal error is not seeing those mistakes once you have done them."

Watts insists that a good composition starts with a good idea. It must be well composed, well drawn, and made up of good shapes—the overall shapes that form the picture. It should be dramatically lit and with a full scale of values. Historical accuracy, technical accuracy, and/or degree of detail can enhance the effect, but are not the primary components.

Watts suggests starting with mentally imagining the scene. Consider how weather, light, values, and shadows will enhance the scene. Repeat this process for several arrangements.

Gather photographs of the aircraft that have been selected and include photographs that might give additional arrangement possibilities. Gather cloud and background photo references appropriate to the respective arrangements. Clip and file reference material often for just such planning purposes.

Work up a series of simple thumbnail sketches. (Watts uses Prismacolor gray markers with a fine and broad tip on one pen that keep an artist from getting too fussy about detail.) Watts said, "Get the darkest dark down and let the white of the paper work for highlights. Prevent the markers from becoming muddy by using a good grade rag marker paper that doesn't bleed."

Once a good composition is established, use a tracing paper overlay to experiment with background and cloud shapes. Select two or three thumbnails to enlarge to preliminary drawings, perhaps to 8.5 inches by 12 inches. This is the stage that determines whether the composition is worthy of becoming a painting. When the picture has good composition, pleasing relationships, shapes, balance, and believability, Watts said, "Go back to reread the rules. If the picture has none of the pitfalls, do a fairly tight drawing. When satisfactory, have that drawing Xerox-enlarged on bond paper to the final size, preserving the exact relationship of all the elements. On good quality vellum, overlay the enlargement and do a finished detail drawing."

Watts has created a list, a Basic Rules of Composition, with the admonition, "Violate at your own risk." Among his basics, he suggested avoiding the following: tilting the horizon and the subject in the same direction, yet recognizing that, when nothing is parallel to the edge of the page, action is implied; intersecting the aircraft with anything approaching a 90-degree angle; too many similarly sized, similarly shaped (excepting a formation of aircraft), and similarly spaced objects (trees, clouds, and so forth); and overcrowding.

Compositions have the chance of success when:

- an artist starts with a good premise, a believable image, and good composition,
- a full range of values is used,
- perspective is correct,
- the picture is well and imaginatively lighted,
- the elements are linked through value and placement,

- good shapes are selected,
- hard and soft edges are appropriate,
- atmospheric perspective exists,
- a sense of movement exists, and
- a sense of drama exists.

Learn to draw with these concepts in the back of your mind. Check the basics again after your composition is nearing completion.

Watts added, "There are no shortcuts. If you follow this somewhat rigorous approach, you will be doing better work than you thought possible."

AVOIDING PITFALLS

As with any artistic endeavor, there are mistakes to be avoided. Learn to watch for them as you are learning to draw and avoid having your later paintings fail. Here are a few:

• Avoid bad tangencies.

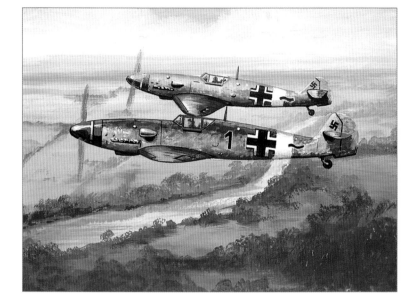

◄ Among the pitfalls to be avoided are bad tangencies—the contact of a line, curve, or surface touching but not intersecting another. One aircraft's wingtip should not exactly touch the top of the canopy of an adjacent aircraft in formation. The lower edge of the vertical stabilizer and rudder should not align with a row of trees in the distance below. Don't allow a paint stripe on the fuselage of an aircraft to match the width and location of a stream meandering far below. Don't allow the spinner on the propeller to abut a distant road or vertical line. ©Andy Whyte, ASAA

• Be careful that vertical objects do not stop the movement and action of your drawing. Use vertical lines to convey strength. Use horizontals to express action and motion.

↙ Horizontal lines contribute to forward motion, diagonals give the illusion of speed. Vertical lines, especially those that intersect the dominant subject, bring an abrupt halt to the action you are trying to portray. This B-24 Liberator seems to be stopped in midair. ©Andy Whyte, ASAA

↓ Avoid creating lines directly to the corners of your image. They will draw the viewer's eye away from the scene. Avoid having any part of the dominant subject just touch the edge of the paper. See that overlapping subjects clearly overlap. ©Andy Whyte, ASAA

• Lines drawn directly to the corners of your drawing will carry your viewers' eyes out of the scene. Have nothing point directly toward any corner of the drawing. Do not place objects just touching the sides of the drawing. Any object that overlaps another should clearly overlap.

• Avoid including similarly shaped objects that are the same size and that are evenly spaced.

➤ Similarly shaped objects of the same height and evenly spaced from one another should generally be avoided. Aircraft flying in formation or parked in a line on an airfield ramp are an exception.
©Andy Whyte, ASAA

• Beware of inaccurate perspective, often brought on by excessive reliance on photographs. Take a second look at the F6F Hellcat in chapter 5.
• Be diligent and accurate in doing your research homework, in depicting the correct movement and position of aircraft control surfaces, and in showing the way light illuminates aircraft surfaces. Look again at the B-24 Liberator in chapter 3, at the Mustang and Spitfire in chapter 1, and at the "mystery plane" in chapter 5.

THUMBNAIL SKETCHES

Remember this as you quickly create thumbnails: a good composition starts with a good idea and is well composed, dramatically lit, and well drawn. There is no focal point if all of the objects of your composition are exactly the same size. The elements of your composition—its key shapes—must be placed well in relation to one another.

The effective use of thumbnail sketches, as described in chapter 4, Sketching and Line Drawing, will be of great value in preparing your composition and in avoiding the pitfalls outlined. They need not be detailed, but there is a critical need for enough of them to prove to yourself that your good idea has been well presented in a balanced way, that it uses a full range of values, and that it has successfully avoided the pitfalls that make drawings fail. Again, there is no substitute for hard work and practice in drawing!

Golden Mean, a Pleasing Proportion

Andrew C. Whyte, ASAA

In discussing how to give compositions their best proportions, Andy Whyte explained the Golden Mean. He said, "Although the following information should not be used slavishly, it is worth consideration. A study of artworks of all genres—paintings, sculpture, pottery, and architecture—revealed that the best proportions were found in what have been attributed to the Golden Mean.

A natural phenomenon, there is a rich geometry to the proportions of the Golden Mean, as seen in the diagram. Starting with a single rectangle there is a natural sequence of nested rectangles obtained by removing the leftmost square from the first rectangle, the topmost square from the second rectangle, and so forth. This results in a spiral, a shape often found in nature.

The Golden Mean can also offer a pleasant proportion to a painting if one *divides* the canvas with balance and counterbalance. Henry Poore suggested a simple division in his book, *Composition in Art*. On a rectangular canvas, connect two opposing corners with a diagonal. From this diagonal, connect one of the remaining corners with a line that is perpendicular to the diagonal. Through a point on the diagonal where it is met by this perpendicular line, draw two straight lines connecting each side of the rectangle and meeting the sides of the rectangle at right angles. The divisions that result are excellent bases for construction. In addition, they each in turn can be divided by the same means. The painting composed within these Golden Rectangles will offer the most balanced proportions possible.

By dividing and subdividing a canvas to these proportions, the ratio remains the same in each subsequently smaller rectangle and all of the rectangles can be connected by a smooth and interesting spiral. There is a rich geometry to the Golden Mean and, when used as the basis for a composition, the viewer's eye is drawn into the artwork with the same dynamic and rhythmic circulation as the symmetrical and beautiful spiral that is the Chambered Nautilus.

Test this theory of balanced proportion in paintings that have stood the test of time and have become classics. Artists may not have consciously chosen to use the concept of the Golden Mean, but, nonetheless, have created compositions that bear out the principle.

During the early 1930s, the Johnsons were the first wildlife photographers. They used two Sikorsky Aircraft, S-38 and S-39, for their explorations of Africa and Borneo. Andrew Whyte's painting shows the lines of analysis described by Henry Poore. Note that the center of interest, the photographers Martin and Osa Johnson, falls exactly at the division of the painting and the balance and counterbalance of the dominant and subdominant shapes that complete the composition.

"Every color or hue has a range of values. Every color has an intensity. Those are what you play with in color work." *Andy Whyte, ASAA*

COLOR

To Understand Color, Understand Value and Intensity

Light is the source of color. Light, with its waves of electromagnetic energy, interrelates with the surfaces it illuminates and, with the human eye, can be translated into a hue or color that we can recognize and name. Light, with its spectrum of differing wavelengths, reflects differently from the objects or surfaces it touches. It is that reflection from the visible spectrum that appears to the eye as color. In the absence of light, there is no color. In the absence of light, there is no shadow. Use light to direct interest to the most important part of your drawing or painting and learn to use it sparingly and effectively.

Colors have important qualities and can elicit a variety of emotions. Those that contain yellow or red are warm colors. They seem to be solid, to advance toward us, and to expand in size. Cool colors are those that contain blue. They seem to be spacious, to withdraw from us, and to contract in size. Color has three basic properties: hue, value, and intensity.

HUE

Hue refers to a particular color, such as red, blue, or yellow. An artist's color wheel, a tool derived from the natural colors of a rainbow, aids in visualizing colors and their relationships. As black and white are not shown on a color wheel, it is important to know that, in pigment, the absence of color results in white, and black is the combination of all colors.

Primary colors are those colors that cannot be mixed from other elements. Traditionally, those colors have been red, yellow, and blue; modernization has identified the three primaries as magenta, yellow, and cyan. The secondary, or complementary colors, are those colors that result from the mixture of two of the primary colors.

A complementary color is one of two colors whose mixture produces gray. The mixtures of red with green, yellow with violet, or blue with orange all produce gray. Depending upon what you want to paint and which side of gray you want, you can mix those with warmer and cooler results. For example, mixing a French ultramarine with cadmium yellow results in a bluish gray, a cooler gray. On the warmer side, you can create a more orange-colored gray.

It is important to know that complementary colors accentuate one another's hues—a spot of green near a red makes the red look redder, for example. As complementary colors have very different wavelengths, when painted next to one another they can seem to quiver. When two colors are mixed in pigment, they lose some intensity. When two colors are mixed optically, they retain intensity or can even seem brighter.

BURNT UMBER - DARK RED greyed
LAMP BLACK - BROWNISH
IVORY BLACK - NEUTRAL
PAYNES GRAY - MIXTURE OF BLACK + ULTRAMARINE

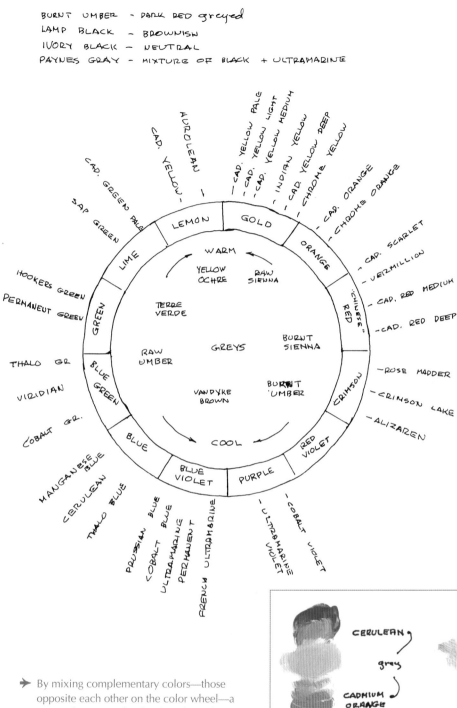

This special and personal color wheel developed by Andy Whyte provides a great deal of information in addition to that found on a standard color wheel. Around the exterior circle, he has shown the names of the colors of oil, acrylic, and watercolor paints. These names often reflect the chemical composition of a color. For example, cadmium yellow is cadmium sulfide and cobalt blue pigment consists of a mixture of cobalt oxide and alumina. Note the information shown, inside the wheel, about mixing colors to create grays.

The following color notes also apply: Depending on the area of a painting each color covers with respect to an adjacent color, the colors can change or appear to the eye to have a different tint. A good rule of thumb is to have large areas of muted color contrasted with smaller spots of intense color.

• Red next to orange, makes red seems purple and the orange more yellow.
• Red next to green and blue makes both colors brighter.
• Red next to blue makes red seem orange and blue seem green.
• Orange next to green makes orange appear red and green seem blue.

By mixing complementary colors—those opposite each other on the color wheel—a range of grays can be developed. Cooler and warmer grays can be obtained by mixing the right hues.

The following color charts are valuable exercises for an artist to perform in the personal development of his or her understanding of hue (color), value (light and dark), and intensity (saturation or chroma). To be valuable, these should be considered hands-on exercises. You have to work them; they cannot simply be studied.

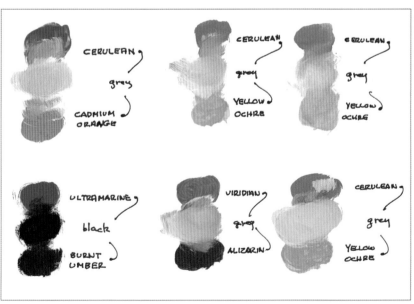

Knowing the location on the color wheel of the paints that you use is important. Accurate color mixing has three steps:

1. Select the color closest to the one you want to use. Mix from adjacent hues, if necessary.

2. Add a little of the hue's correct complement to achieve the desired intensity.

3. Add a touch of white to adjust for value.

VALUE

Value is the range in a single color from darkest—a value of one—to lightest. Some hues, such as yellow or orange, are relatively light in value and others, like purple and brown, are relatively dark. Yet, as do the lightest of hues, the darkest—purple and brown—also have an entire range of values. In differentiating between the darkness or lightness of a particular color, we label those differences as shade and tint. Shade is the relative darkness—a low value on our value scale—and tint refers to the relative lightness—a high value.

Value change can occur gradually, darkening as the object is distanced from the illuminating light. Even if the object is white, there will be value differentiation from a lighter white to a darker white. Note that a color adjacent to the object being drawn will influence the value of that object.

Every color, right out of the tube, has a value. Some manufacturers note that value on the tube of pigment itself. It is up to the artist to lighten or darken it to change the value of the pure hue for his or her painting. An artist can tint a hue to lighten or can shade a hue to darken the value of any color.

Shadows are opposite light sources and occur because an object blocks the light. This will cause color changes in the area of shadow. Remember to lower a color's value in any portion affected by the cast shadow. A good example is seen in the F-86 Sabre in chapter 9.

INTENSITY, SATURATION, OR CHROMA

Intensity, also called saturation or chroma, refers to a color's purity. A color with the greatest saturation has the greatest purity of tone. It can be grayed to change the intensity from the purest (maximum) to medium to weak, the least intense. The amount of intensity desired for a particular object in a composition is the artist's choice. In drawing and painting aircraft, atmospheric interference normally causes a diminishing brightness with distance. Colors have a greater intensity when they are closer to a viewer. Softening the intensity can cause objects to recede with diminishing saturation to enhance the atmospheric quality and give depth to a painting. Aerial perspective adds the ability to use

Quote

Color has three basic properties; hue, value and intensity."

color, value, and intensity to create depth with a graying of color and/or a loss of value and intensity with distance.

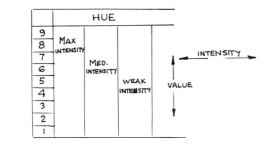

COLOR IN PAINTS

Professor Albert H. Munsell created a color order system that made the description of color accurate and convenient. Munsell published *The Atlas of the Munsell Color System* in 1915 and his system served as the foundation for other color order systems that have followed.

Start adding color to your drawings with an array of colored pencils and pastels. When you are ready to start painting, choose paints that will best serve your needs.

Watercolors

Watercolors are generally acknowledged to be the most challenging medium to undertake. Watercolors rely on applying one or more layers of translucent color. Watercolor paper, with its texture and its differing visual appeal, is an integral part of the finished painting. With watercolors, there is immediacy to the painting; it is less forgiving of mistakes, changes, or erasures.

Acrylics

Acrylics are water-soluble and quick drying through the evaporation of the water solvent. That quick-drying quality can be extended through the use of a retarder. Acrylics can be applied in various thicknesses and to various surfaces. They are durable; they can be diluted and therefore are ideal for airbrushing. They retain flexibility and will not yellow with age. When allowed to dry rapidly, successive coats can be applied within a half-hour and the finished painting is waterproof and less apt to deteriorate. Acrylics are the choice of many aviation artists, especially those who face short deadlines.

◄ This diagram provides an overview of the two color charts that follow. Here, value ranges from 9 at the top—the lightest—to 1 at the bottom—the darkest. (Other books may label values differently—be aware.) Each of these charts has the hues arranged from left to right. For each hue, there are three intensities.

▼ The two color charts are arranged as outlined in the diagram. For your exercise, start by mixing each color, at full intensity, for each of the nine values. Then reduce the intensity in two steps—to medium and weak intensity—at the same value. Satisfying yourself that you have built a "perfect chart" will take patience and practice. The learning that takes place will make it worthwhile.

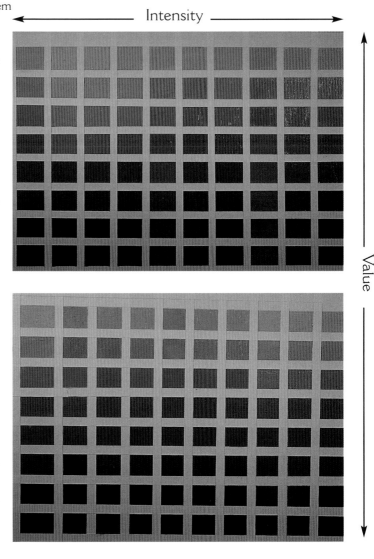

Intensity

Value

➤ The chart with two spheres also has exercises to help you develop your understanding of value, intensity, and soft edges. The sphere on the left—in yellow—is an exercise in value. It goes from the lightest light to the darkest dark through a full range. The sphere on the right applies color in corresponding values and reduces in intensity as you move toward the edges of the figure. The soft edges help to create the illusion of roundness. The surface on which the sphere rests has the same value from front to back; the color is reduced in intensity to make the surface appear to "lie down." ©Andy Whyte, ASAA

Oil Paints

Oils are opaque or semi-opaque and have long been the choice of classic artists for their relative ease of use and great variety of effects. Because oils dry slowly, tones are more easily matched and blended. The artist can apply paint that is based in linseed, poppy, or walnut oils in glazes, washes, spray, impasto, and with a palette knife. Design can be changed and improvised and color and shading offer rich effects.

There is no need for a beginning artist to rush into the purchase of a full array of prepared colors. Some aviation artists use limited palettes. Keith Ferris uses a basic three-color palette with white. Robert Watts uses a basic five-color palette with white. Andy Whyte uses that same five-color palette, using cobalt blue instead of pthalo blue. Part of the art of painting involves seeing and training your eyes to color differentiation—the exercises in this chapter are intended to help you do this. Training your eyes to color is as important as perfecting your ability to see the subjects you wish to paint. When you create your colors from a limited palette, you are training your eyes to see color.

Although most artists would agree on the differentiation between red, yellow, and blue, color itself is highly subjective. It becomes a matter of personal choice for an artist to select pigments. Remember that several colors can be found in one object—some of it the actual color of the object and some of it caused by the reflections of other colors. The challenge to the artist is to discover all of the colors that are actually present in objects to be painted.

In creating your paintings, learn to link elements together through your judicious use of color. Make certain that, for drawings and paintings of aircraft, you learn to create atmospheric perspective and practice giving less color definition to those objects that are in the distance in your scene. Never forget that the basis to all good paintings is good drawing.

Color Just One Aspect of a Painting

Kristin Hill, ASAA

Kristin Hill, trained and skilled in fine arts, is an Artist Fellow of and has served as an officer of the American Society of Aviation Artists. She is an active participant of the U.S. Air Force Art Program. Acutely aware of the world around her, Kristin noted, "Visual clues never cease. Research is available everywhere—light, shadow, color, transparency, reflection. Artists work with a visual language as composers work with a musical language."

Hill uses work boards—flats that contain reference photographs, sketches, color samples, mechanical drawings, and models for referral during a painting—that can be quickly stowed to free her to work on another painting. She explained, "I like to have several paintings going at a time so that I can put one down and look at another. The eye physiologically reaches a certain saturation of color and the intense concentration focused on a painting has to be eased once in a while."

In order to view her work in progress each time she refreshes her brush with paint, Hill keeps her palette 6 to 8 feet from the painting. She said, "The artist whose job it is to see and produce needs to see more."

School's Out Early

The simple concept inspiring her painting *School's Out Early* lies in the excitement generated by early aviation's barnstormers. Having met a contemporary pilot who enjoys flying a Travel Air, Hill selected his aircraft paint scheme for her painting. A second Travel Air owner made his craft available to her—for photographs, to study, to absorb the sounds, odors, and in which to enjoy the sheer pleasure of flight.

Beginning with thumbnail pencil sketches to try a variety of compositions, Hill established the general view of the craft, its flight energy, and the placement of relative values and light and shadow. Selecting the best, the sketch was expanded to a larger format in which she developed the relative placement of values more thoroughly. A rough color sketch followed that fitted the components of the painting to one another and could be changed quickly if necessary. The color sketch was designed to bring together harmoniously the colors, values, composition, aircraft view, energy, and rhythms.

School's Out Early required using a three-view drawing and descriptive geometry to plot the desired view and proper structure of the Travel Air. Hill then created the play of light and color on its shapes and used linear perspective to draw the buildings and aerial perspective to assure the illusion of flight. In addition to observation of the human figures from the open cockpit aircraft, she watched people below from the vantage point of a 12-story building, seeking all the time to insure the accuracy of her perspective.

A Brush with Gold

During the 50th anniversary of the U.S. Air Force, Hill elected to paint a tribute to the McDonnell-Douglas F-4 Phantom, to its long and respected history of service, and to those persons who were involved. Having previously had "an impressive flight experience in which the clouds were illuminated from a sun that cast light below them," she drew upon a pen sketch and notations of that scene for this painting.

Hill developed her composition with thumbnail sketches that explored masses and force-lines, and followed the quickly executed thumbnails with a color sketch. She said, "Separate, yet one with this fluctuating world in the sky, is the beautifully piercing passage of man and machine. . . . The strong and sculptural shapes of the F-4—and the relative positions of sun, cloud, and aircraft—allowed the light to strike the F-4 and its contrail. Placing the shadowed cloud beneath the Phantom emphasized the sunlight and the painting of 'gold.' This painting is an example of visual music."

The Importance of Color

Robert Watts, ASAA

Color is one of the tools in mastering the illusion of space and distance. To use color successfully, gain a working knowledge of values, edges, shadows, and light. Here are some of Robert Watts' cogent pointers:

Values

•Values are the lightness, which advances, or darkness, which recedes, of the shapes and elements of a painting.

•Use as few values as possible to describe a form.

•When an object recedes into space, its value should be similar to other values at the same distance.

•Save the darkest dark and lightest light for the center of interest.

Edges

•Edges should soften and become less distinct with distance. This deliberate loss of focus is something we want the viewer to notice less. If the distance is the center of interest, the foreground objects should be less sharply defined.

•Fact: The eye will always focus on the cleanest, sharpest thing it sees. What happens when everything is clear and distinct? That's right, no center of interest!

Four P-47 Thunderbolts with D-Day Invasion stripes over the Netherlands. *©Robert Watts, ASAA*

Shadows

•Shadows give structure to a painting.

•Shadows are where we find our darkest darks, one aspect of a full range of values.

•Shadows should look vague and mysterious, *not* full of information.

•Paint shadows with subtlety. Don't draw undue attention to them.

•Opacity is the look of light. Shadow is transparent. To increase the transparency, add a bit of yellow or orange to the shadow. Yellow is the color of transparency.

Douglas A-4 Skyhawk catching the wire on the carrier deck.
©Robert Watts, ASAA

Light

• The center of interest is in the light or silhouetted against the light.

• If you have a lot of light, take out some of the color. Don't have color and light competing.

• You can never paint your lights too light or your warms too warm. You can always darken or cool them later, but the opposite is more difficult.

Warm and Cool Colors

• Cool colors have blue in them and warm colors have yellow in them.

• Confusion comes from using a palette of too many colors. Use a palette that contains only those colors you really need.

• White will cool any color and should be used sparingly.

• It is easier to cool a warm than it is to warm a cool. Paint warms first; add cools carefully.

• The eye is drawn to yellow, orange, and red. It sees cool colors only peripherally.

• Warm colors advance toward the eye while cool colors recede from the eye.

Complementary Colors

• Darken a yellow by adding purple or darken a purple by adding yellow.

• Create your darkening complements out of cool colors for the shadow side and warm colors for the lighted side.

• Make lively grays by mixing complementary colors.

Local Color

• Local color is the actual color of an object if it were unaffected by any others.

• Local color is usually affected by two sources of light: the sun, warm and yellow, and the reflected light of the sky, cool and blue.

• Local color is usually clear only on an overcast day when neither warm sun nor cool blue sky can have much effect.

Color

• Either put color in one place or de-emphasize color in another place. It is color against the lack of color.

• All three primary colors should never be in the same picture in their full intensities.

• To make something look bright, use more color, less white.

• To make something look lighter, use less color, more white.

• The color of light falling on a scene will and must modify all colors and unify the picture.

• Warm color has a transparent nature and conveys the look of depth in a shadow. Yellow is the color of transmitted light.

• Reserve your most intense colors for the lighted areas.

• Put your color on the canvas and leave it alone. Fussing with it causes chalkiness and the well-known muddiness in the darker tones.

• Try and use a selected color again and again in your painting so that your painting will hold together. If you need a dark, use one that you have already used. Avoid fragments of arbitrary color."

CREATING PAINTINGS

Aircraft As an Inspiration—A Modern Art

"There are no 'tricks' involved in painting. Some beginning artists think that all they have to do is learn 'tricks' from a professional and their job is made easier. That is simply not true." *Andy Whyte, ASAA*

Why paint aircraft? Have you always loved things that fly? Have you spent time doodling pictures of airplanes on the edges of your school papers? Do you enjoy building aircraft models? Are you fascinated with aircraft of all types and with their beauty and speed?

If your answers are, "Yes," you share many qualities with the world's best aviation artists! With few exceptions, all of them started with a deep interest in flying, eyes that scanned the skies at the sounds of overhead engines, model aircraft building, and drawings that might have distressed their schoolteachers. If only those teachers could see them now and recognize the successful artists they have become! Just like you, they share a deep reverence for the mystery and the awe of flight and of the exploration of outer space.

A good painting grows out of and develops from the intent of the artist. Now that you are working at your skill in drawing aircraft, hone in on the skills that need to be developed to create aviation paintings.

AVIATION IS YOUNG

Most of us forget that the airplane has been with us for a relatively short time—the 100th anniversary of the birth of powered flight is December 17, 2003. To see impressionistic paintings of World War I aircraft painted by the French landscape and portrait artist Henry Farré is to take a historical look at the initial impact of aviation. Those who draw aircraft, thanks to their acute observation skills, are valuable in portraying moments in time that otherwise would be lost to history entirely.

Aviation and the chance for people to fly brought a new way of viewing the world—a bird's-eye view. Although landscape artists had long used shape, line, color, tonal values, and texture to produce sensations of light, this new way of viewing the world from a great height added impetus to finding ways to show vast reaches of space, atmosphere, speed, and motion. This opened a new artistic career field and created opportunities for those who love drawing and painting aircraft.

TOOLS FOR PAINTING

As we've cautioned before, it is not necessary to purchase a great deal of expensive equipment. You will need some brushes. For detail and to create sharp edges, a bright brush has short flat bristles. For rounded and softer edges, a round brush has a round barrel and staggered lengths to the bristles. To create soft and diffused edges, a filbert is shaped with a slightly rounded edge. A flat brush, with long flat bristles, is useful for long fluid strokes and strong edges. Finally, a fan brush can contribute to your soft edges and subtle blending techniques. Synthetic bristles work with synthetic pigments; but when working in oils, always use natural bristles.

A palette is a flat, thin board on which paints can be mixed. The surface should not adversely affect the quality of the paints and, for ease of cleaning, should be easily scraped with a palette knife or razor. A palette knife can be used for mixing paints and for applying paints to your canvas or board surface for impasto effects.

Collect a supply of rags with mineral spirits, solvent, or water for the inevitable cleanup. Rags, too, can be used to blend and soften edges on the painting itself.

PIGMENTS

Choose your tools and select the pigments that will offer you the results you want—oils, acrylics, or watercolors. Although you can later choose to stretch your own canvas or linen over stretcher bars, start with prepared canvas-covered boards or wood panels to which either an oil or an acrylic gesso is applied to the surface prior to painting. As acrylic paints will not adhere to an oil gesso, acrylic gesso can be a good choice as a ground for both acrylic and oil paints. Acrylics tend to be less glossy than oils. Also, oils maintain their color throughout the drying process while acrylics have a semi-opaque look while wet that becomes transparent after the drying process. Only experience will help you to anticipate the appearance of the finished color.

SAFETY CONCERNS

When you start painting, choose a ventilated area, have access to a window that can be opened, and consider the use of an exhaust fan. Try to situate your painting area in a different location than the rooms in which you and your family members eat and sleep, and keep your painting area as clean as possible. Avoid smoking, eating, and drinking while you are handling paints. If you plan to use hazardous materials and aerosols, wear gloves and use a mask over your mouth and nose. Keep your hands clean after you have been painting and wash your painting clothes or smocks separately from other laundry. Some paints contain toxins that are hazardous to your skin or can be hazardous if breathed. Keep safety a primary concern.

START WITH THE PRELIMINARIES

Start with thumbnails, sketches, and an initial drawing. Make several studies and create a drawing, focusing on the composition, proportions, perspective, and tonal values. When you have achieved the work

Quote

"A good painting grows out of and develops from the intent of the artist."

that pleases you, transfer that drawing to the canvas or panel with a light pencil, charcoal, or a thin wash of a neutral color. Some artists use a translucent tracing paper, some project the drawing onto the surface to be painted, and some draw freehand after having divided the drawing via a grid system that helps to keep the shapes accurate.

Limit your color choices. By mixing your own grays, browns, and other earth tones, you will be able to better manage your cool and warm colors and avoid the prospect of muddy results. Choose the palette of colors and remember that complementary colors will liven one another. Don't underestimate the power of negative space. Seek balance in your composition and in your choice of colors.

Rather than concentrate on drawing firm edges to outline your objects, allow background color to meet the color of the object and shape the form without a line. Pay attention to your source of direct light and to the reflected light. Make certain that your darkest tonal values and lightest tonal values are found in your center of interest.

In oil painting, drying time can be speeded with the addition of drier or solvents. Conversely, drying time can be slowed with the use of oils as the thinning agent.

In layering either acrylics or oils on the surface, use the thinner, faster-drying additives for the undercoats and use the slower-drying combinations for the outer layers. In concentrating on your center of interest, be sure that you don't neglect the other portions of the canvas.

Try to get your aircraft to seem to soar or to move through the surrounding air. If it looks as if you can cup your hand behind your aircraft, you have successfully created that important distance, space, and atmosphere that is inherent in the world of flying and in the realm of aviation art. As renowned artist Robert Grant "R. G." Smith has written, "I liked to put an airplane in the picture, not on it."

A PAINTING IS CREATED

To bring together all of the information from previous chapters, Andy Whyte has chosen an incident that took place during World War II. He has prepared a description and the drawings that show a step-by-step process that can be used to create a painting of this particular historic event. Andy brought together research material, thumbnail sketches, descriptive geometry layouts, a value sketch, a color rough, and final paintings—one each in watercolor, acrylic, and oil.

RESEARCH

Based on interviews with the pilots involved with the incident, Andy learned that, during the U.S. invasion of the island of Okinawa, the Japanese launched intensive kamikaze attacks on the Navy ships

Quote

"If you want to draw aircraft like a pro, you must DRAW, DRAW and DRAW. Have fun while you're at it."

supporting the landings. One of the U.S. fighter squadrons charged with foiling these attacks was VMF-222, a Marine Corps unit equipped with F4U Corsairs. Lt. Bill Harford served as a pilot in this unit under Capt. Ken Walsh. On June 14, 1945, Lieutenant Harford was preparing to fire on a Mitsubishi "Kate" torpedo bomber diving to make an attack on the fleet when Captain Walsh went in for the "kill."

The pilots gave Andy the valuable description of the mission, the weather conditions, and the time of day. Andy went to the books to gather descriptive data, including scale drawings and photographs of the U.S. and Japanese aircraft, and other background information.

THE HUMAN FACTOR

As you become more adept at painting your favorite machines—aircraft—you will notice that no aircraft operate without a cluster of humans around and in them. Make an effort to learn to draw humans from life, using models to pose in different stances to capture the nuances of the human figure in three dimensions. Using chiaroscuro to define different planes of the human body, identify your light source and choose: highlight, light, shadow, core shadow, reflected light, secondary highlight, and the cast shadow.

Virtually all lines in the human body are gently sweeping curves. When using a model, improve your drawing skills by drawing single parts—the hand, the arm, or the torso, for example. Also practice sketches that focus on particular areas of tension in the human form that indicate gestures—the folded arm, the outstretched hand. This practice enhances your powers of observation.

Practice applying linear perspective to the figure to delineate the changes that occur when limbs reach forward and

▼ Thumbnail Sketches
Six rapidly sketched drawings were done to evaluate shapes, values, and composition.

➤ **Descriptive Geometry**
Having selected the sketch to be used,
Andy prepared descriptive geometry layouts
to insure the correct linear perspective for
the three aircraft involved in the scene—
two F4U Corsairs and the "Kate."

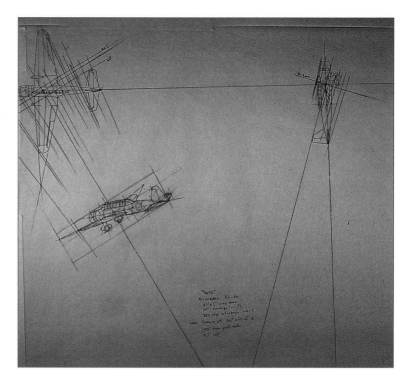

◄ **Pencil Sketch**
Andy next prepared a large pencil sketch to establish values
in the foreground, middle ground, and background. This
sketch also helped with the establishment of the horizon
and the light source.

◄ **Color Study**
To move from black and white, Andy prepared a color
"rough," a study that helped him validate the lighting and
the values.

must be foreshortened. Foreshortening is a technique that you will use often in correctly depicting the airfoils of aircraft and the same perspective applies to the human figure that is running toward the viewer or moving away. It is a method by which an artist can add depth and drama and show a figure at various angles.

Learn, too, the muscles of the human body and the skeletal armature that gives shape and form. The more you know, the better prepared you are to correctly depict the human form and the other aspects of the scene. Several artists are known for their excellent drawings featuring human involvement in aviation. Study their works.

GETTING STARTED IN AVIATION ART

How do you establish a reputation as an aviation artist? When asked, most artists would suggest:

- Start small.
- Have faith in your ability.
- Be willing to put in the hard work that it takes to succeed.
- Do your homework. Prepare a portfolio that demonstrates your best work.
- Give yourself time to grow in skill.
- Begin with small goals. Produce.
- Work on quality.
- Acquaint yourself with other artists and join a group like the American Society of Aviation Artists (ASAA)—a group to which you can contribute and with which you can communicate, learn, and grow.

Many accomplished artists have tales of perseverance, of determination, . . . and a bit of luck. Your curiosity sparked your motivation to learn to draw aircraft. That is the spark that attracted the masters of the genre and kept them interested and creative. Learn from them and continue to work at your drawing and your painting. Enjoy what you see and what you translate into a work of art. Don't give up. Keep trying. Keep DRAWING.

⬆ Final Paintings
For the purposes of this book, Andy has prepared three finished paintings of the scene over Okinawa—one in watercolor, one in acrylic, and one in oil. The results of his careful research and thorough preparation are apparent in each one.

Developing a Painting

Richard Allison, ASAA

This sequential series of sketches and slides by ASAA Artist Fellow Richard Allison show the development of a 20-by-30-inch oil painting. The scene depicts a Nakajima B5N2 "Kate" over "battleship row" during the Japanese attack on Pearl Harbor, December 7, 1941.

Allison, an art teacher and an award-winning artist, spent a stint in the U.S. Army. He has worked extensively in pencil drawings and has considerable experience in alkyd media and with oils. He has been quoted as having said, "The mark of a successful aviation painting is how aircraft and nature complement each other. Artwork with a blank or indifferent background becomes only a rendering. A painting consisting of aircraft and environment harmonized in an effective composition is true aviation art."

Starting with thumbnail sketches, he establishes the correct perspective through descriptive geometry. To create his painting and to describe the sequence simply, Allison listed the following steps, documented in slides:

Line drawing of the "Kate" placed over the ships.

Water blocked in, using a combination of viridian and burnt umber.

Deck painted in and hulls refined. "At this point, I include the black in the aircraft's engine. This is the darkest part of the painting. It helps me visualize the values by giving me a reference point to keep the battleships distant."

Blocking in the aircraft.

The finished painting.

A Mighty Fortress

Jody Fulks Sjogren, ASAA

A true "pro," Jody Sjogren got her start as a medical illustrator and she has carved her very special niche as an aviation artist with her two print series, Metamorphosis and Metaphor. The focus here is on her *Metaphor II: A Mighty Fortress*. She has very generously described her process for "creating a piece of artwork that has a symbolic message that happens to involve an airplane."

To help an artist understand the complexity of the "synthesis of design" involved in the creation of this painting, Jody has outlined her step-by-step procedure. She explained, "I am trying to draw a historical parallel between the knights on warhorses of medieval times defending the empires of their lords and the men who fly armored warhorses of modern times. A deeper message, though, relates to the continu-

Metaphor II: A Mighty Fortress. ©Jody Fulks Sjogren, ASAA

al conflict in the invisible spiritual realms where God's strength triumphs over the forces of darkness."

To get started: "I use the nature, structure, or mission of an airplane as the starting point for my composition." To develop a "personal relationship" with the plane, she reads extensively, interviews crew members, takes lots of photographs, and, when possible, arranges a flight. In this case, she credited the words of retired USAF General John Shaud, who talked her through "the history of the Cold War and the role of the B-52 as one who had flown it for many years."

To gather resources, Jody visited Barksdale AFB, Louisiana, a major B-52 home base, to develop her relationship with the Stratofortress. She attended a Renaissance Festival in Ohio to, "aim my camera at some real live knights and warhorses." She pointed out, "The keys to these research forays are an open mind, a sharp eye for action, and a limitless supply of film."

Back in the studio with her gathered resources, she begins the sketches. She noted that, "Early in the game, it's rare that I have all of the information in hand and all of the visual problems solved in my mind. Thumbnail sketches are a part of the process of solidifying my message as well as working out a visual composition." For A Mighty Fortress, many detailed sketches followed. All were discussed with and critiqued by knowledgeable friends and it wasn't until the seventh one—a sketch that eliminated what one pilot called a "confusion in the visual geometry"—that the final composition was decided upon.

This seventh sketch began to pull it together with the B-52 "on launch" and the knights, symbolic of the crew, moving in the same direction—departing the fortress. The smoke trails from the eight jet engines merged with the dust kicked up by the horses and the clouds that surrounded the fortress. These "provided the 'visual glue' that I needed to tie all of the elements together successfully."

The final sketches focused on the knights and the horses and added symbolism to provide the connectors to the B-52 crew members of today—helmets, squadron insignia, and the Strategic Air Command patch. The specific B-52 depicted is Old 1040, the final B-52H off the assembly line; it is the youngest B-52 in service today.

With "all of the big decisions and most of the small ones made," it is time to paint. Jody transferred the final sketch to her Strathmore five-ply Bristol board for the full-color painting. She said, "I work on a kid-finish, 100 percent rag surface that takes very readily the mixed media technique—airbrushed watercolor, washes, and Prismacolor pencil—that I use. I start with light washes of watercolor and of Prismacolor first, gradually working into the darker layers as I define the shapes and details." Jody described this stage of the process as "long and patience-trying." She stays with it, however, because the finished effect is pleasing to her and to the many who collect her work.

She says, "I know I'm finished when I like what I see and there's nothing more to do. Knowing when to stop is almost as important as getting a good start."

Design, Color, and Intricate Paintings

James Dietz, ASAA

Attributing the observation to the prestigious British artist, the late Frank Wootton, James Dietz said, "Too often aviation artists are concerned only with painting an accurately detailed aircraft, yet overlooking two very important principles of painting—design and color. An artist must always remember that no amount of detail or attention to the proper number of rivets can correct a boring situation or a flat composition.

"A realistic painting is composed of the basic elements of design, color, and accuracy to life. From an artistic standpoint, the least important of these is accuracy because it is the most easily corrected. Somewhat harder, but not impossible, to correct is color. But, if the composition and design are not exciting to the viewer, no amount of accuracy can make up for it. Of course, this is the most difficult element to achieve."

Bon Chance

World War I has been of great interest to Jim Dietz. His approach celebrates human participation in aviation and has helped to expand the genre of aviation art. In *Bon Chance*, World War I British pilots and crew members stride past French farm buildings. En route to their planes, parked in the pasture that serves as their aerodrome, they are facing aerial combat beyond the front lines. Dietz has created an intriguing contrast between the young warriors, determined and courageous, yet uncertain of their fate, and the pastoral farmyard that buzzes with the activities of everyday existence. Dietz brings his story to the viewer and invites participation and response. His art succeeds when a viewer can't help but become involved.

Note the attention to detail in preliminary and completed paintings. These details have become a hallmark of Dietz's fine art.

Once all the preliminary research has been completed and the situation decided upon, Dietz starts with thumbnail sketches that are done quickly and yet with enough accuracy to confirm the strength (or weakness) of the composition. They include most of the detailed information gained from the research and, occasionally, he submits these to experts in the field to confirm that his composition is reasonably accurate. He said, "If so, great—but, if not, a corrected sketch may be required."

He progresses to a nearly full-sized pencil sketch. "By the time the drawing is transferred to stretched canvas," he said, "all the technical problems have been solved (I hope), the composition has been nailed down, color has been worked out in a color sketch, and all that is left to do is to paint. I usually work from thin transparent underpainting to more and more opaque layers with a minimum of surface development or impasto."

Dietz's paintings capture single moments in time. Emphasizing the personal involvement in aviation, he re-creates the interaction between humans and machines. Time and again the viewer is drawn into each painting, investigating something not previously noticed or becoming involved in the scene.

GALLERY OF ARTISTS

THE SPIRIT OF FLIGHT

Mark Pestana

This painting of the B-2, *Spirit Over Edwards*, was commissioned and the customer required that the B-2 be shown over the site at which it was flight-tested, Edwards Air Force Base (AFB), California. The customer also required that the T-38 chase plane, the main runway complex, and Rogers Dry Lake be included.

The artist, Mark Pestana, was free to create an artistic arrangement for the composition, with no specific requirements as to direction of flight, time of day, altitude, or particular weather conditions. Although the upper Mojave Desert region is generally noted for its clear and dry air and relatively low incidence of clouds and moisture, Pestana chose to add a series of high-altitude cirrus sweeps, complementing the sweeping lines of the bomber and its chase plane.

In addition to the research required to accurately depict the two aircraft, the artist used maps and aerial photographs of Edwards AFB and the surrounding dry lakebeds. Edwards AFB and Rogers Dry Lake are crisscrossed with numerous runways. The main runway, 04 and 22, and its parallel counterpart are asphalt and shown as black lines. The other runways are outlined in asphalt. Pestana is a Lieutenant Colonel in the USAF Reserve, stationed at Edwards AFB. He flies from the base, giving him the opportunity to actually witness the scene as well as the B-2 in flight—a great asset to correctly depicting the aircraft.

THE DRAMA OF FLIGHT

Domenic DeNardo, ASAA

Domenic DeNardo, formally trained in art and in engineering, is a pilot who uses the platform of the cockpit for repeatedly viewing the light, shadow, atmospheric perspective, and aerial reference as background for his art. In 1995, piloting his Beech Bonanza, he joined 131 other Bonanza pilots for a memorable formation arrival at the Experimental Aircraft Association's annual AirVenture Fly-In and Convention in Oshkosh, Wisconsin. The gathering of so many Beech aircraft inspired an award-winning painting.

Focusing on the drama in flight and translating the sunlight and its shadows to his art, DeNardo has painted, in *Departure From Ice Station Ruby*, the stark Greenland icecap and a departing LC-130D of the 109th Airlift Wing of the New York Air National Guard (NYANG). The workhorse of the sky, this Lockheed C-130 is equipped with the necessary skis for the repeated landings and takeoffs that are required by the NYANG's commitment to flights onto the Greenland ice to resupply necessities to those maintaining the DEW line radar stations of the arctic. In his preliminary drawing and the finished painting, DeNardo has captured the moment in time in which the craft lifts off of the ice to return to its home base in Schenectady, New York.

STORY TELLER

Jack Fellows, ASAA

The aviation art of Jack Fellows, Artist Fellow member and former president of ASAA, is storytelling at its finest. Whether the stories are part of his Cactus Air Force Art Project, the extensively researched and beautifully painted documentation of the World War II air war in the Pacific, or of other twentieth century aerial warfare campaigns, they spring from a single motivation. Fellows, and his research director, Bob Rocker, are seeking to record as many eyewitness narratives of the pilots, aircrew, and ground-based support personnel involved in these campaigns as possible. They are especially concerned with stories of outstanding bravery that have received little in the way of deserved publicity and recognition.

Once the narratives have been recorded, the stories are extensively researched for verification and additional detail. If the story lends itself to a visual presentation, Fellows begins with a series of study drawings and paintings that he "checks out" with the eyewitnesses and historians for accuracy. When the research and the preliminary images all come together, Jack does a large oil painting of the historical event, paying special attention to the terrain, the fortifications, and the atmospheric conditions that played a role in making the event significant. Those paintings have illustrated a number of unit histories, several books, a large collection of stamps, and have gained international recognition in art shows and exhibitions. The four shown here are just a few of Jack Fellows' stories, well documented for posterity and created in tribute to the warriors who lived them.

Lockheed P-38 Lightning, tail number 43-28776, flown by Ben Mason, commander of the 82nd Fighter Group, dive bombs the oil field at Ploesti, Rumania, on June 10, 1944.

Jack Fellows

Republic P-47 Thunderbolt performing an armed
reconnaissance mission against a German supply train
in France during the summer of 1944. The pilot was
Ralph Jenkins, commander of the 510th Fighter
Bomber Squadron.

The F-111A Aardvark had its baptism under fire in Vietnam in 1968 during Operation Combat Lancer. Here, on the fifth operational sortie for the controversial swing-wing jet, a target near Vinh is destroyed and the aircraft climbs to altitude. The pilot was Detachment Commander Ivan Dethman and the Weapons System Officer was Rick Mattheis.

The pilot of a German Focke-Wulfe 190D approaches the airdrome at Flensburg, Germany. The field has been overrun by British forces in April 1945 and the pilot is preparing to surrender himself and his aircraft.

133

THE IMPRESSION OF FLIGHT

Luther Gore

uther Gore became interested in creating free-flight gas model airplanes and devoted several years to creating an air force of flying
models. Gore said, "The hand-eye coordination developed by creating
models cannot help but assist an artist in heightening his knowledge of
the shape and form of aircraft, a good start toward drawing."

Gore is more interested in creating scenes of a nostalgic era than a
particular moment in time. He said, "Aviation of the past is believed to
have been more heroic, more glamorous, and more easily fathomable in
its moral dimensions than aviation of the present. . . . The British artist John
Young once told me that, 'if you feel that you can reach your hand around
in back of an airplane in a painting, then the illusion of flight has been
achieved.' I would like to paint in an apparently effortless style that would
result in creating that illusion of flight. The effortlessness would be a sign
that I had absorbed spiritually what flight is all about and then 'said it all'
with a few choice strokes on canvas—from the soul to the brush in one fell
swoop. I know that giving the appearance of having simply plopped paint
down is a trick that takes enormous discipline and a great deal of practice."

Sailors

In *Sailors,* Gore has linked the romance and the
lure of the sky and of the sea. In a soft, painterly
style he depicts a sailboat on quiet waters, seeking
the air that will give motion to the craft, in harmony
with the balloon that depends upon that same flow
of air to give action to its flight.

Looking for Subs

Having studied the work of the "Father of Aviation Art," World War I artist Henry Farré, Luther Gore chose to
paint in the loose impressionist style of the French portraitist who served as a combat artist. Choosing a
French FBA flying boat on patrol with a British destroyer as his subject, Gore consulted several World War I
books to get an idea for a naval scene. He generalized the concept of an anti-sub operation in the Atlantic.
He said, "I wanted the airplane to be the central point of interest, hence the somewhat darker values in the
wing and tail shadows, which also have the effect of moving the airplane somewhat closer to the viewer
than the ship. I also wanted to try a Farré treatment of the billowing clouds and the choppy seas below."

135

VIETNAM

REMEMBERED

Wilson Hurley,

ASAA

On January 23, 1968, in the midst of the war in Vietnam, U.S. President Lyndon B. Johnson ordered the activation of reserve units. Members of New Mexico Air National Guard's (ANG) 188th Tactical Fighter Squadron (TFS) of the 140th Tactical Fighter Group (TFG) responded, among them was then-Maj. Wilson Hurley, a pilot of the 188th TFS.

Called a "Landscapist of Grandeur," Wilson Hurley is an internationally known artist. After having studied military topography, graphics, and mechanical drawing, he flew for the Army in the Philippines, for the New Mexico ANG, and as a Forward Air Controller (FAC) in Vietnam. Each experience taught him to make a conscious effort to commit to memory much of the surrounding environment as research for his art. He uses acute powers of observation to indelibly etch in his mind the remarkable colors, shapes, and actions of scenes seen from the air.

Hurley brought from the grueling conflict in Vietnam a series of remembered wartime experiences.

Continued on page 139

Air Strike in "Happy Valley"—"Happy Valley" was just east of Anh Khe pass. Here troops in contact are sending up red-and-green smoke to mark their positions and the FAC has sent in his white phosphorous rocket marking the target for one of a flight of two F-100Cs from the Iowa ANG squadron stationed at Phu Cat. The F-100 is carrying high drags [bombs] and unfinned napalm [containers of jellied gasoline] used in low-level skip bombing and is also armed for strafing with four cannons. Each pass of each fighter will be cleared by the FAC, who is in radio contact with his air support team and the ground commander.

Wilson Hurley

Working a Pair of "Tacos" North of Checkpoint Pecker—TACO was a call sign of the New Mexico ANG at Tuy Hoa. The terrain is common to the central highlands of Vietnam north of the Kylo River. The fighter's pylons [mounts for bombs] are empty and the second fighter is pulling up from his last pass in the distance as the leader flashes by the FAC heading home. On the ridgeline are the fires of a friendly patrol.

Hurley exhorts an artist, before starting to draw, to know where the sun is, to know the condition of the sky, to note the color of the surface, if any, under the object being drawn, and the location of shadows and reflections. He said, "When you find a painter who puts the entire surround of his universe into that painting, I'll show you a painter who ends up in the National Gallery or the Metropolitan. A painter who forgets that or thinks it unimportant is always wondering why he never gets as far along as he thinks he should."

Air Strike at the French Fort—Ten kilometers west of Tigertown in the central highlands of Vietnam there are the remains of a triangular French fort built in the Viet Minh days. On the evening of the first day I reported to my forward location, we were in contact with the North Vietnamese and conducting air strikes close to the fort. My boss, Maj. Ed Garland, took me out in the back seat of an O-1 [aircraft] to observe the strikes that were being controlled by Maj. Norm Comfort. We arrived just as an F-4 Phantom had a can of napalm explode on his wing. I thought he had been shot down, and the vivid scene etched itself on my memory. As it turned out, the F-4 flew through the fire unscathed.

FLYING IN THE EARLY DAYS

John Paul Jones

In 1919, Gen. Billy Mitchell, then Assistant Chief of Air Service and Director of Military Aeronautics, designated Fort Bliss, El Paso, Texas, as an air terminal. He created an armed aerial reconnaissance designed to support cavalry and infantry troops. This was the start of the first Army Border Air Patrol of the U.S./Mexico international border. Twelve de Havilland DH 4 biplanes left Houston, Texas, to fly to El Paso, a dangerous cross-country flight that resulted in eight safe landings, one fiery, fatal crash, and three nonfatal crashes. These Border Patrol "Red River Pilots" flew Liberty-powered biplanes over desolate mountains with unpredictable turbulence and winds, and over the barren desert, an unforgiving terrain that offered little in the way of landing sites, water, or fuel.

With imaginative vision that surpassed that of other men of his era, Billy Mitchell found success with the Border Air Patrol. Using a cavalry target range north of Fort Bliss, he equipped the aircraft with 25-, 50-, and 100-pound bombs and tested his concept of aerial bombing. This led directly to his innovative and controversial experiments with the bombing of obsolete battleships in the coastal waters of Virginia.

John Paul Jones has painted one pastel, *DH 4 – U.S. Air Service,* and a watercolor, *Way Out West,* that document the hazardous and heady days of early military aviation. Having met a participant, Jones wanted to tell the Border Air Patrol's story and wanted to involve his viewers in that story.

In pencil, Jones has drawn the SPAD XIII and has included a pencil detail drawing of his scene. With only pencil on paper, the artist shows his ability to create atmospheric perspective, light and shadow, and an illusion of depth and distance.

A multi-engine rated commercial and charter pilot, Jones has flown numerous aircraft. He said, "Having flown them, I can paint them with just a little more intensity. Just as an airplane seems to come alive in a pilot's hands, I want my art to generate the same degree of vibrancy and emotion."

DH 4 – U.S. Air Service

John Paul Jones

Way Out West

SPAD XIII

AN ARTIST NEVER STOPS LEARNING

John Clark, ASAA

John Clark, an artist fellow member and past president of the American Society of Aviation Artists (ASAA), credits his study of perspective to Keith Ferris as the catalyst for his method of drawing. He assisted in the painting of Ferris' famed *Fortresses Under Fire*, the mural in the World War II Gallery of the National Air & Space Museum, Smithsonian. From Ferris he learned the technique of descriptive geometry, and he also learned of and entered the USAF Art Program.

As others have said, "There are no shortcuts to learning to draw." John Clark not only recognizes that truism, he practices his art and continually strives to improve. When he became committed to an art career, he recognized that there is no room for complacency. The art of drawing and painting requires a lifetime of study and work.

Having earned a bachelor's degree in fine art, a master of art, and a master of fine arts in drawing and painting from the University of Wisconsin, Milwaukee, Clark continues to be a consummate student and continues to strive for excellence. He is known for his attention to and knowledge of the great masters of fine art, and he has never let that study flag. He studies and analyzes contemporary artworks as carefully as those of the past. When he begins to create one of his own paintings, he uses descriptive geometry and works to achieve precision as well as beauty.

Interested in the realism of aerospace art, Clark studies great art as avidly as he researches the scientific and technological data. He has been quoted as having said, "To a painter, there's more to it than just presenting planetary landscapes and a starry background. You have to fall back on the history of art and the works of great landscape painters. It involves how you look at a scene and present its different elements in artistic terms."

John Clark used mathematical descriptive geometry to work from his initial idea for a painting to the finished work, *Saturn From Tethys*. ©*John Clark, ASAA*

John Clark

↓ *Commercial Aviation,* John Clark's award-winning painting of a Boeing 737-200 airliner,
demonstrates his attention to perspective.
Having completed the precise drawing, he
completes his painting. Using a limited palette
of color, he creates an ethereal atmosphere that
surrounds the passenger jet. ©*John Clark, ASAA*

AN ALASKAN MORNING

Priscilla Messner Patterson

In response to a commission from the Aircraft Owners and Pilots Association (AOPA), Kodiak resident and artist Priscilla Messner Patterson answered the request for a holiday greeting card that included a floatplane, cabin, mountains, and snow. Most of those elements are easily found in Alaska. "Except," said Priscilla, "it is not uncommon for the lakes and inland waters to be frozen. Many aircraft are put on skis, wheel-skis, or Tundra tires for the winter."

Priscilla found a cabin at Blue Fox Bay on Afognak Island in the Gulf of Alaska. Accessible by salt water, the site offered the elements of winter, snow, and mountains, as well as moving water and an aircraft that continued to wear its floats. She located photographs of an actual cabin on the shore of the moving water, although it was hidden by tall evergreens that surrounded it. The cabin was also at too great a distance from the water to include a floatplane, even at high tide. Her artistic license allowed her to move the cabin closer to the shore, to heighten its importance by changing its front door from brown wood to a yellow, and to brighten the windows with a warm and welcoming interior light. She completed the holiday mood by decorating the door with a festive swag of greenery tied with a red ribbon. Each of Priscilla's preliminary sketches brought her closer to the final drawing selected for delivery to the client.

Backlighting the cabin with early morning light and creating a forested, snowcapped mountain, she debated whether the plane would look better dragged up onto the lightly snow-covered beach or as though a pilot had just arrived for a holiday visit. Knowing that most floatplanes would be more intricately and safely tied down for a long-term stay, she opted for a short-term visit and tethered the floatplane to a large rock on the shore. She titled her painting *Peaceful Morning*.

LOOKING FOR THE SHAPES

Michael O'Neal

Michael O'Neal has earned a well-deserved reputation as a scholarly researcher and first-class aviation artist. His highly accurate paintings of World War I in the air have been recognized with three consecutive Thornton Hopper Awards presented by the League of World War I Aviation Historians. They have also earned top honors at the *SimuFlite/FLYING* magazine's "Horizons of Flight" exhibition, EAA's Annual Sport Aviation Art Competition, and the American Society of Aviation Artist's James Roy Award for Best In Show.

O'Neal's painting of the U.S. 95th Aero Squadron's Nieuport 28 resulted from some work as an amateur detective that uncovered a history lesson. Given a German-made postcard showing the Nieuport with the appropriate 95th markings, he was stunned to see the U.S. pilot's body stretched out on the ground beside it. The postcard was clearly intended as a propaganda piece, but the downed pilot was not identified. O'Neal set out to learn who it was and why the enemy had created postcards of this particular pilot.

Tracking back in time, O'Neal meticulously researched into squadron records that dated from the time the 95th Aero Squadron transitioned from Neiuports into Spad XIIIs. He was able to establish that the downed pilot was Quentin Roosevelt, the youngest of former President Theodore Roosevelt's four sons, all of whom were in U.S. service in "The Great War."

Continued on page 152

U.S. 95th Aero Squadron's Nieuport 28

Micheal O'Neal

Continued from page 150

Delving further, he was able to learn that young Roosevelt had been on patrol in the Nieuport on July 14,1918, when he became separated. Spotting three other airplanes that he mistakenly took for his squadron mates, he joined up with them. Imagine his shock when he discovered that the airplanes belonged to the enemy!

Roosevelt continued to close in and managed to shoot one down before he was shot down and killed. O'Neal's painting is an artistic tribute to the U.S. warriors who volunteered to fight for freedom—in France and in French aircraft that were greatly outnumbered.

For his award-winning painting *Sharks*, O'Neal chose to depict the disciplined and aggressive German aviators in a tight formation of Albatros D IIIs. Although the Germans were using a variety of aircraft late in the conflict, O'Neal focused on the Albatros because of its shark-like shape. Picking up on artist Paul Rendel's emphasis on shapes, O'Neal said, "Shapes are the whole reason that a picture captures your attention from a distance—not the subject, but the shape in the composition."

In discussing *Sharks*, O'Neal allowed that, even with the basic shape chosen, the composition wasn't easy. "I drew form after form, watched for tangencies, negative space, interesting things going on. I didn't like any of them."

"Then I returned to the original concept and started all over again. I wanted it to look organized, disciplined, and aggressive, and it needed a good shape!"

O'Neal worked until his composition pleased him. As winner of "Best Of Show," it obviously pleased many astute judges of art and a myriad of viewers as well.

For his award-winning *Sharks*, O'Neal performed a series of steps from silhouetted shapes, to rough sketch, to thumbnails, to pencil drawing, and to painting of *Sharks*.

GLOSSARY

Acrylic: Water-soluble paint made from pigments and a plastic binder.

Aerial or Atmospheric Perspective: Creating a sense of depth in drawing or painting by imitating the way the atmosphere makes distant objects appear less distinct and more bluish or grayish than they would be if nearby.

Aquatint: An etching technique in which a solution of asphalt or resin is used on the plate. Aquatint produces prints with rich, gray tones.

Caricature: An artwork humorously exaggerating the qualities, defects, or peculiarities of a person, an idea, an object, or a machine. *Aerocatures*™ are the copyright of Hank Caruso.

Cartoon: A humorous sketch or drawing usually telling a story or caricaturing a person or action. In fine arts, a cartoon is a preparatory sketch or design for a picture or ornamental motif to be transferred to a fresco or tapestry.

Carving: In sculpture, the cutting of a form from a solid, hard material such as stone or wood, in contrast to the technique of modeling.

Casting: In sculpture, a technique of reproducing a work by pouring into a mold a substance, such as plaster or molten metal, which then hardens.

Chiaroscuro: The rendering of light and shade in painting; the subtle gradations and marked variations of light and shade for dramatic effect.

Collage: A composition made of cut and pasted pieces of materials, sometimes with images added by the artist.

Colors, primary, secondary, complementary: Primary colors are red, yellow, and blue, the mixture of which will yield all other colors in the spectrum but which themselves cannot be produced through a mixture of other colors. Complementary colors are two at opposite points on the color scale—for example, green and red, orange and blue, purple and yellow. Secondary colors are produced by a mixture of two primary colors—for example, orange (a mixture of red and yellow), green (a mixture of yellow and blue), and purple (a mixture of red and blue).

Composition: The organization of forms and colors within an artwork.

Drawing: The technique of making lines, figures, and pictures as with a pencil, pen, or brush on a surface.

Drypoint: A technique of engraving, using a sharp-pointed needle, that produces a furrowed edge resulting in a print with soft, velvety lines.

Engraving: The art of producing printed designs through various methods of incising on wood or metal blocks, which are then inked and printed.

Etching: The technique of producing printed designs through incising on a coated metal plate, which is then bathed in corrosive acid, inked, and printed.

Figure: A representation of a human or an animal form.

Foreshortening: Reducing or distorting in order to represent three-dimensional space as perceived by the eye, according to the rules of perspective.

Fresco: Meaning "fresh" in Italian. The technique of painting on moist lime plaster with colors ground in water.

Frieze: A band of painted or sculpted decoration, often at the top of a wall.

Genre Painting: A realistic style of painting in which everyday life forms the subject matter, as distinguished from religious or historical painting.

Gesso: Ground chalk or plaster mixed with glue and used as a base coat for tempera and oil painting.

Gouache: A method of watercolor painting that is prepared with a thicker base (more glue-like) and produces a less transparent effect.

Highlight: On a represented form, a point of most intense light.

Horizon Line: In perspective, this represents the line in nature where the sky appears to meet the earth.

Impasto: Paint applied very thickly. It often projects from the picture surface.

Landscape: A drawing or painting in which natural scenery is the subject.

Linear Perspective: A mathematical system for creating the illusion of space and distance on a flat surface.

Lithography: A printing process in which ink impressions are taken from a flat stone or metal plate prepared with a greasy substance, such as an oily crayon.

Modeling: In sculpture, the building up of form using a soft medium such as clay or wax, as distinguished from carving. In drawing and painting, using color and lighting variations to produce a three-dimensional effect.

Monochrome: A drawing or painting executed in a single color.

Monotype: A single print made from a metal or glass plate on which an image has been represented in paint, ink, etc.

Mural: A large painting or decoration done on a wall.

Oil: A method of painting with pigments mixed with oil, producing a vast range of light and color effects.

Orthogonal Lines: Straight diagonal lines drawn to connect points around the edges of a picture to the vanishing point. They represent parallel lines receding into the distance and help draw the viewer's eye into the depth of the picture.

Palette: A flat board used by a painter to mix and hold colors, traditionally oblong, with a hole for the thumb; also, a range of colors (limited or extensive) used by an individual painter.

Pastel: A soft, subdued color; also, a drawing stick made of ground pigments, chalk, and gum water.

Perspective: A method of representing three-dimensional volumes and spatial relationships on a flat surface to produce an effect similar to what is seen by the eye.

Polychrome: A painting using a variety of colors.

Polyptych, diptych, triptych: In painting, a work made of several panels or scenes joined together. A diptych has two panels; a triptych has three panels.

Realism: The style of art in which the artist strives to make the painted scene look as real and natural as possible.

Relief: In sculpture, the projection of an image or form from its background. Sculpture formed in this manner is described as high relief or low relief (bas relief), depending on the degree of projection. In drawing or painting, the apparent projection of parts conveying the illusion of three dimensions.

Stenciling: A method of producing images or letters from sheets of cardboard, metal, or other material from which forms have been cut away.

Still Life: The representation of inanimate objects in drawing, painting, or photography.

Tempera: A painting technique using pigments mixed with egg yolk and water. Tempera produces clear, pure colors.

Texture: The visual and tactile quality of a work of art based on the particular way the materials are handled; also, the distribution of tones or shades of a single color.

Three-Dimensional: Having height, width, and depth. A box is three-dimensional.

Two-Dimensional: Having height and width only. A painting of a box is two-dimensional.

Tone: The effect of the harmony of color and values in a work.

Tortillion: A soft gray paper spiral wound tightly to a point at one end. Tortillions, or stumps, are used to blend pencil, charcoal, pastels, and other artist medium for shading and tone.

Value: The degree of lightness or darkness in a color; the scale from darkest dark to lightest light.

Vanishing Point: The single point in a picture where all parallel lines that run from an object to the horizon line appear to come together.

Wash: A thin layer of translucent color.

Watercolor: Painting in pigments suspended in water. It can produce brilliant colors and transparent effects. See: **gouache**.

Woodcut: A print made by carving on a wood block, which is then inked and printed.

BIBLIOGRAPHY

Books

Blake, John, G.Av.A., and Ohn Hellings, G.Av.A. *Members Instructional Manual*. London: The Guild of Aviation Artists, 1998.

Caruso, Hank. *Seabirds, An Unofficial Illustrated Encyclopedia of Naval Aviation*. Charlottesville, Virginia: Howell Press, 1995.

Cooper, Ann L., with Dorothy Swain Lewis. *How High She Flies*. Arlington Heights, Illinois: Aviatrix Publishing, 1999.

Daugherty, Charles, Editor. *How To Draw*. Danbury, Connecticut: Famous Artists School Cortina, 1954.

Fargis, Paul, Editorial Director. *The New York Public Library Desk Reference*. Third Edition. New York City: Simon and Shuster Macmillan Company and The Stonesong Press, 1989, 1993, 1998.

Ferris, Keith. *The Aviation Art of Keith Ferris*. New York City, Toronto, London: A Peacock Press/Bantam Book, 1978.

Hebblewhite, Ian. *The North Light Handbook of Artists' Materials*. Cincinnati, Ohio: Writer's Digest Books, 1986.

Hurley, Wilson. *Wilson Hurley, A Retrospective Exhibition*. The Lowell Press of Kansas City, 1985.

McCall, Robert. *The Art of Robert McCall*. New York City, Toronto, London: Bantam Books, 1992.

Kerschner, William K. *Advanced Pilot's Flight Manual*. Ames, Iowa: Iowa State University Press, 1976.

Parramón, José María, Course Director. *The Basics of Artistic Drawing*. New York City: Barrons, 1994. First edition, *Las Bases del Dibujo Artistico*. Published in Spanish, 1992.

Poore, Henry Rankin. *Composition in Art*. New York: Dover Publications, 1976.

Ruskin, John. *The Elements of Drawing*, with notes by Bernard Dunstan. New York: Watson-Guptill Publications, a division of BPI Communications, 1997. Originally published by The Herbert Press Ltd., 1991.

Smith, Robert Grant, and Rosario "Zip" Rausa. *The Man and His Art, R.G. Smith, An Autobiography*. Atglen, Pennsylvania: Shiffer Military History, 1999.

Taylor, Thom, and Lisa Hallett. *How to Draw Cars Like a Pro*. Osceola, Wisconsin: MBI Publishing Company, 1996.

Turner, Michael. *Drawing and Painting Racing Cars*. Sparkford, Somerset, U.K., Haynes North America, Newbury Park, California: Haynes Publishing, 1999.

Whitney, Richard W. *Painting the Visual Impression*. Stoddard, New Hampshire, 1995.

Magazines and Magazine Articles

Caruso, Hank. *Aerocatures*™ Calendar for 1999. California, Maryland: *ForeFeathers Enterprises*, 1999.

Dietz, James. "Jim Dietz, EAA Master Artist." *Sport Aviation*, September 1998.

Doherty, M. Stephan, Editor-In-Chief. *Art Methods & Materials*, An American Artist Publication, New York City: BPI Communications , 2000.

Hurley, Wilson. "Asymmetrical Thrust." *Aero Brush*, Newsletter of the American Society of Aviation Artists, Vol. 7, No. 1, Winter 1993–1994.

Thompson, Charles. G.Av.A., ASAA, MGMA. "The Circle in Perspective." *Aero Brush*, Newsletter of the American Society of Aviation Artists, Vol. 13, No. 4, Fall 2000.

Watts, Robert. "Putting the Picture Together." *Aero Brush*, Newsletter of the American Society of Aviation Artists, Fall 1995.

Watts, Robert. "Color Principles for Successful Paintings." *Aero Brush*, Newsletter of the American Society of Aviation Artists, Vol. 10, No. 1, Winter 1996–1997.

Magazine Articles Written by Ann L. Cooper:

Burrows, Paul. "Artist's-Eye View." *Private Pilot*, Vol. 26, No. 5, Ma 1991.

Cohen, Gil. Quoted from his talk at the 8th Annual Forum ASAA, American Airlines C.R. Smith Museum, Dallas/Fort Worth, Texas. *Aero Brush*, Newsletter of the American Society of Aviation Artists, Vol. 7, No. 3, Summer 1994.

Cohen, Gil. "Art of Flight." *Aviation (History)*, July 1993.

Cooper, Ann. "Getting Started in Aviation Art." *Aviation Illustrated*, Vol. 1. No. 1. January 1996.

Ferris, Keith. "The Precise Painter." *Private Pilot*, Vol. 25, No. 9, September 1990.

Gore, Luther. "Henry Farré, The First Aviation Artist." *Aviation Illustrated,* Vol. 1, No. 2, August 1996.

Gore, Luther. "Getting Started in Aviation Art." *Aviation Illustrated*, Vol. 1, No. 1, January 1996.

Galloway, Nixon. "The Beauty of Flight." *Private Pilot*, Vol. 28, No. 12, December, 1993.

Hill, Kristin. "The Missed First Flight." *Private Pilot*, Vol. 25, No. 12, December 1990.

Hurley, Wilson. "Eye for Painting," *Private Pilot*, Vol. 26, No. 11, November 1991.

McCall, Robert. "Solar Power from Space." *Aviation Art Showcase*. Vol. 1, No. 1, Fall 1995.

Phillips, William S. "Eye of the Wingman." *Private Pilot*, Vol. 24, No. 8, August 1989.

Phillips, William S. "Landscapes, Skyscapes, and Aerial Machines." *Aviation Illustrated*, Vol. 1, No. 1, January 1996.

Rendel, Paul. "Artcraft." *Private Pilot*, Vol. 26, No. 9, September 1991.

Rendel, Paul. "Getting Started in Aviation Art." *Aviation Illustrated*, Vol. 1, No. 1, January 1996.

Watts, Robert. Quoted from his talk at the 8th Forum ASAA, American Airlines C.R. Smith Museum, Dallas/Fort Worth, Texas, 1994.

Whyte, Andrew C. "Art of Flight." *AVIATION*, March 1994.

Websites

American Heritage® Dictionary of the English Language, Third Edition. New York: Houghton Mifflin Company, 1996. Electronic version licensed from INSO Corporation. www.ohio/ink.edu/db/ahd.html

Encarta, 98 Online Encyclopedia. Microsoft Corporation 1996–97. www.encarta.msn.com

International Museum of Cartoon Art, http://cartoon.org/about.htm. A collection of 160,000 cartoons, including: animation, comic books, comic strips, gags, editorial cartoons, greeting cards, caricature, graphic novels, sports cartoons, illustration, and computer-generated art.

Larmann, Ralph M. *Art Studio Chalkboard*. Indiana: University of Evansville, Internet, 1998. www.evansville.edu/studiochalkboard

INDEX

Abstract, 102
Acrylics, 111, 117, 118
Adobe Illustrator, 38
Adobe Photoshop, 38, 39
Aerial perspective, 73
Aerocatures™, 84–89
Aerodynamics, 22
Ailerons, 22, 26
Airbrush, 36, 38
Airfoil, 20, 21, 26, 27
American Society of Aviation Artists (ASAA), 51
Background, 91
Backlighting, 94
Blimps, 23
Breitling Orbiter, 23
Bright brush, 116
Brush pen, 37
Carbon pencils, 34
Carbon sticks, 34
Cartoons, 84–89
Cartridge paper, 35
Caruso, Hank, 87–89
Cast, 51
Cast shadow, 93
Center of Gravity (CG), 21, 22
Center of interest, 80
Charcoal, 35
Chiaroscuro, 92
Chroma, 110
Color rough, 118
Colored Pencils, 34
Complementary colors, 108, 115
Compound forms, 74
Contour, 52, 89
CorelDraw, 38
Crosshatching, 49, 81
Cutaway drawing, 76, 77, 82
Da Vinci, Leonardo, 24
Deneba's Canvas, 38
Depth, 54, 62, 65
Descriptive geometry, 67, 70
Dip pen, 37
Direct lighting, 92
Dirigibles, 23
Distance, 62, 92
Drag, 20, 26
Drawing interiors and cockpits, 79
Edges, 114
Ellipse. 48, 72, 74
Erasers, 34
Fan brush, 117
Felt tip pen, 37

Felt-tipped marker, 37
Ferris, Keith, 51
Fiber pen, 37
Filbert, 116
Flaps, 26
Flat brush, 117
Foreground, 91
Form, 49, 92
FreeHand, 38
Geometric layout, 118
Geometry, 89
Gliders, 25
Golden mean, 101, 107
Graphite pencils, 34
Graphite sticks, 34
Helicopters, 24
Highlights, 49
Horizon, 101
Horizontal, 51
Hot air balloons, 23
Hue, 108, 109
Human models, 59
Impressionistic, 102
Ingres paper, 35
Intensity, 108–110
International Space Station, 25, 31
Jasc Paint Shop Pro, 38
Jones, Brian, 23
Lateral axis, 72, 74
Lift, 20, 26
Light source, 90
Light, 51, 80, 89, 115
Line Drawing, 49
Linear perspective, 62, 64
Local color, 115
Macromedia, 38
Main focal point, 99
Major axis, 72, 74
Materials, 22
Mathmatical perspective, 62
Middle ground, 91
Minor axis, 72, 74
Model aircraft, 58
Montgolfier Brothers, 23
Natural light source, 91
Oil painting paper, 35
Oils, 112, 117, 118
Outline drawing, 58
Overlapping, 91
Palette knife, 117
Palette, 117
Pencil drawing, 79

Pencils, 34
Perspective drawing, 62
Perspective projection, 67
Perspective, 62, 91
Physics, 89
Piccard, Bertrand, 23
Picture plane, 62, 65, 68, 69
Pitch, 20, 21
Pose, 89
Prismacolor, 34
Proportion, 62
Propulsion, 22, 27
Reflected light, 90, 92
Reservoir pen, 37
Roll, 20, 21, 22
Round brush, 116
Rubbing, 49, 81
Saturation, 110
Scale drawing, 78
Secondary colors, 108
Secondary light source, 92
Shading, 48, 49, 81
Shadow, 49, 51, 52, 80, 90, 114
Sikorsky, Igor, 22, 24
Single-point perspective, 62, 63
Sketchpads, 34
Sketching pencils, 34
Sketching, 47
Slots, 26
Spaces, 51
Station Point, 62, 68, 69
Structures, 22
Subordinate points, 99
Surface, 89
The Atlas of the Color System, 111
Three-point perspective, 64, 80
Thrust, 20, 26
Thumbnail sketches, 106, 117, 118, 119
Tints, 49
Tonal plan, 102, 103
Tonal Values, 54
Two-point perspective, 63, 64
Value sketch, 118
Values, 51–53, 90, 91, 108–110, 114
Vanishing Point, 62, 63, 65, 68, 69, 72, 74, 94
Vellum, 35
Vertical measuring line, 69
Warm and cool colors, 115
Watercolors, 111, 117, 118
Weight, 20, 26
Wright Brothers, 22
Yaw, 20, 22

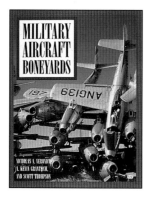
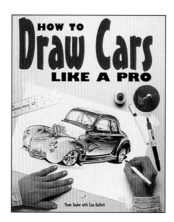

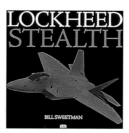